AF424501

How This Book Can Help You Hack Growth
In the quest for growth, simplicity is often the key to scalability. This book serves as a roadmap for those who aspire to achieve exponential growth in their personal and professional endeavours. Designed as a self-help guide, its primary aim is to provide clarity on how you perceive your business or relationships and empower you to unlock your full potential. Through brain mapping exercises, akin to conducting an MRI scan of your brain, you'll gain profound insights into your beliefs and perceptions.

1. Clarity Through Brain Mapping:
The book introduces you to the concept of brain mapping, a powerful tool for gaining insight into your thought processes. Through brain map exercises, you'll learn how to conduct an MRI scan of your own brain, gaining clarity on your beliefs, perceptions, and strategies.

2. Personal and Professional Growth:
By delving into the exercises and insights offered in this book, you'll be equipped to design your own path to personal and professional growth. Whether you're a small shopkeeper, a leader of a large corporation, or a professional seeking to advance your career, the principles outlined in this book are universally applicable.

3. Resurrect and Rebuild Relationships:
In addition to business growth, this book also addresses the importance of relationships. By understanding the dynamics of your interactions and thought patterns, you'll be better equipped to navigate and improve your relationships, fostering understanding, trust, and harmony.

This book is a comprehensive guide for anyone seeking to hack growth in their personal and professional lives. Through its practical exercises, insightful observations, and actionable strategies, you'll gain the tools and clarity needed to embark on a transformative journey towards success. Whether you're looking to grow your business, advance your career, or enhance your relationships, this book offers a roadmap for achieving your goals and realising your fullest potential.

Do You Know How to Do It?
Embarking on the journey of growth hacking through brain mapping requires a systematic approach and a commitment to self-discovery. This section of book outlines the steps involved in harnessing the power of brain mapping to gain clarity and unlock growth potential.

1. Draw Brain Map:
Begin by drawing your initial brain map, representing your current thoughts and perceptions about the subject at hand. Be truthful and honest in your depiction, allowing your thoughts to flow freely onto the paper.

2. Do Corrections:
Upon completing your first brain map, take the time to review and analyse it. Identify any areas of confusion, inconsistency, or blockages in your thinking. Make corrections as needed to ensure accuracy and clarity.

3. Draw Second Brain Map:
Once corrections have been made, redraw the brain map to reflect your refined understanding and insights. This second iteration will likely reveal new perspectives and clarity on the subject.

4. Repeat the Process:
Continuously repeat the process of drawing brain maps, reviewing, correcting, and redrawing until you achieve the desired level of clarity. Depending on your needs and objectives, this may involve performing brain mapping exercises fortnightly, weekly, or even daily.

5. Identify Blockages and Work on Strengths:
Throughout the brain mapping process, pay close attention to any recurring blockages or challenges in your thinking. These may indicate areas where further exploration or development is needed. Similarly, identify your strengths and leverage them to drive progress and innovation.

The key to effective growth hacking through brain mapping lies in the commitment to continuous self-reflection and refinement. By drawing brain maps, correcting errors, and seeking clarity, you'll gradually unravel the complexities of your thoughts and perceptions.

With each iteration, you'll gain valuable insights, overcome obstacles, and unlock new pathways for growth and success. Embrace the process with honesty and openness, and let the power of brain mapping make your thinking easy and transformational.

Reason for Writing This Book

The impetus behind writing this book stems from a deep-seated desire to empower individuals to overcome barriers to growth and unlock their full potential. Through my experiences and interactions with countless individuals, I have witnessed firsthand the common struggles faced by people across various aspects of life.

From business owners grappling with stagnation despite having great potential, to professionals yearning for growth in their careers, to married couples navigating the complexities of relationships—these challenges are unique. I observed a common thread: the camouflage of thoughts that hindered progress and clarity.

Driven by a passion for helping others thrive, I embarked on a mission to simplify the complexities of thought processes and provide practical guidance for navigating life's challenges. This book serves as an earnest effort to extend a helping hand to anyone seeking growth and transformation.

By distilling insights gleaned from my experiences and offering simple yet effective strategies, this book aims to empower individuals to clarify their thoughts, streamline their approach, and unleash their inherent potential. Through the power of self-reflection and the transformative tool of brain mapping, readers will embark on a journey of self-discovery and growth.

Ultimately, the reason for writing this book is rooted in a profound belief in the inherent capacity of every individual to achieve greatness. By sharing knowledge, offering guidance, and fostering a supportive community, we can collectively navigate life's challenges and create a future filled with abundance, fulfilment, and success.

Wonders happen when you think simple & efficiently

Wonders happen when you approach life with simplicity and efficiency. Developing a streamlined thought engine is the key to unlocking endless possibilities. While it's tempting to juggle multiple tasks simultaneously, the true magic lies in simplifying complexity. Rather than getting bogged down by intricate plans and conditional statements like "when I have this, then I will do that," embracing a mindset of simplicity and efficiency propels growth. By focusing on what you have and optimising your efforts to achieve your goals, you pave the way for success. Remember, it's okay to be assertive in your pursuits and rough in language, but kindness is the cornerstone of building meaningful relationships. People are drawn to genuine love and compassion, and fostering these qualities not only enriches your personal connections but also fuels your growth journey. Love, indeed, is the catalyst for transformation and the ultimate key to unlocking your full potential.

Everybody work hard but can't grow exponentially

Despite diligent efforts, many individuals find themselves unable to achieve exponential growth. This phenomenon can be attributed to a many factors, including a cluttered cluster of thoughts, a lack of self-belief, the hindrance of false ego, an absence of love, and an inability to forgive. These elements form formidable barriers that impede progress and stifle potential. However, I firmly believe that everyone possesses the capacity to grow, albeit with varying degrees of simplicity and desire. While simplicity is indeed a potent catalyst for growth, it is often the combination of simplicity and a strong desire that drives exponential progress.

Conversely, some individuals may embody simplicity but lack the fervent desire to propel themselves forward, while others may possess great ambition but struggle to embrace simplicity. Striking a harmonious balance between simplicity and desire is essential for fostering sustainable growth and realising one's full potential.

Unique feature of this book

A unique feature of this book lies in its role as a guiding light through the interconnected journey of self-discovery and growth. Drawing from a wealth of experience and introspection, it offers invaluable insights to unravel the intricacies of personal and professional development. By seamlessly weaving together practical wisdom and thoughtful reflection, this book empowers readers to navigate life's challenges with clarity and confidence. Whether you're seeking to unlock your full potential, overcome obstacles, or chart a new course towards success, this book provides the roadmap you need to embark on a transformative journey of growth and fulfilment.

Preface
In the grand tapestry of personal and professional development, one central theme emerges: the concept that personal growth is indeed professional growth hacking. This book serves as a guide to unraveling the intricacies of this interconnected journey, offering insights gleaned from both experience and introspection.

Contents

Chapter 1: Who am I? Know Your Power Centre - Brain Map
Understanding oneself is the cornerstone of growth hacking. Through a detailed exploration of our inner landscape, we uncover our unique power centers – the driving forces that propel us towards our goals.

Chapter 2: How to Develop Your Power Centre
Once identified, these power centers require nurturing and cultivation. This chapter delves into practical strategies for harnessing our strengths and channeling them towards growth and success.

Chapter 3: Be Rough but Kind at Heart
In the pursuit of our objectives, it is essential to maintain a balance between assertiveness and compassion. This chapter explores the delicate art of being firm in our endeavors while remaining empathetic towards others.

Chapter 4: Develop Thought Engine
Our thoughts serve as the engine powering our actions. By honing our thought processes, we can unlock greater creativity, resilience, and problem-solving abilities.

Chapter 5: Grow Your Business with Your Power Centre
Business growth is intricately linked to personal growth. Here, we delve into strategies for aligning our professional endeavors with our inherent strengths, driving sustainable and meaningful growth.

Chapter 6: Spirituality is Key Asset
Beyond material pursuits lies the realm of spirituality, a source of profound wisdom and guidance. This chapter explores the integration of spiritual principles into our personal and professional lives, enriching our journey towards growth.

Chapter 7: No False Ego
Ego can be a barrier to growth, clouding our judgment and hindering our progress. By embracing humility and authenticity, we pave the way for genuine self-improvement and advancement.

Chapter 8: Build Team - You May Love People Without Liking Them
Effective teamwork is essential for achieving collective goals. This chapter explores the dynamics of building and leading teams, emphasizing the importance of collaboration, even in the face of personal differences.

Chapter 9: Love is Key to Growth
At the heart of growth hacking lies love – love for oneself, for others, and for the journey itself. This chapter delves into the transformative power of love in fueling personal and professional growth.

Chapter 10: Forgiveness is Driver for Growth Hacking
Forgiveness liberates us from the shackles of resentment and bitterness, opening the door to growth and renewal. In this chapter, we explore the profound impact of forgiveness on our journey towards self-actualization.

Chapter 11: Growth Hacking - Truthfulness
Authenticity forms the bedrock of growth hacking. By embracing truthfulness in all our endeavors, we foster trust, integrity, and genuine progress.

As we embark on this exploration of personal and professional growth hacking, may we remain open to the transformative power of self-discovery and continuous improvement.

Preface

Personal growth is Professional growth hacking

As the sun rises on another day of possibilities, I extend my warm greetings to you.

How are you today? It's a question we often overlook in our rush through life, but one that holds the key to our well-being.

This book is not a product of theories confined within the pages of academia; rather, it is a testament to real-life experiences garnered through traversing various industries and Researchers to realize their potential to commercialise patents.

Before delving into the depths of growth hacking, let us first acknowledge the importance of connection and empathy in our daily interactions.

Each individual I've encountered has contributed a chapter to this book, embodying expertise in the art of growth hacking. They come from diverse backgrounds, with unique products, research endeavors, and skill sets, yet they all share a common quest for growth hacking – a term that inherently demands an introspective understanding of one's own strengths and an ethical utilization of these strengths to propel growth.

I must express my gratitude to those who have played pivotal roles in shaping my journey. My daughters, Gayatri and Gauri, my wife Shivani, sister-in-law, brother-in-law, for their unconditional support along with spiritual guides, friends, family, and the extensive team at the WeGo Library Foundation, have been sources of inspiration, critique, support, and love. Their collective influence has laid the groundwork for the growth hacking principles explored within these pages.

Every encounter, whether it be criticism or encouragement, has contributed to the scaffolding of growth hacking. From the serene landscapes of Shirdi and Badrinath, Rishikesh, Haridwar, Nashik to the bustling streets of Mumbai and the cosmopolitan hubs of London and Hong Kong, The Hague, Shenzhen, Delhi each locale, has provided invaluable insights and served as a canvas for experimentation.

As we embark on this journey together, let us remain open to the lessons that life presents us, for growth hacking is not merely a profession, but a philosophy woven into the fabric of our existence.

Chapter 1:
Who Am I? Know Your Power Centre - Brain Map

Understanding oneself is the cornerstone of growth hacking. Through a detailed exploration of our inner landscape, we uncover our unique power centers – the driving forces that propel us toward our goals.

Growth Hacking by MRI Brain

First Step – Situation Analysis

Understanding where you stand today is crucial for effective growth hacking. This involves assessing various aspects such as position, feedback, competition dynamics, and internal capabilities.

By conducting a comprehensive situation analysis, you'll gain valuable insights that will guide your growth hacking efforts and help you chart a path toward sustainable success.

To begin with, the situation analysis let's answer a few questions below:

A. Understanding Where does my Business stand today?
B. What do I think of my Business?
C. What do I think of myself?
D. Am I doing it right?

A. Understanding Where my Business stands today?

Understanding where your business stands today involves a comprehensive evaluation of various aspects to gain insight into its current position, strengths, weaknesses, opportunities, and threats. Here's a breakdown of key areas to consider:

1. **Market Analysis**:
   * Assess the current market trends and dynamics in your industry.
   * Identify your target market segments and their evolving needs and preferences.
   * Evaluate the competitive landscape, including direct and indirect competitors.
   * Determine your market share and positioning compared to competitors.

2. Financial Health

* Review your financial statements, including income statements, balance sheets, and cash flow statements.
* Analyze revenue trends, profit margins, and expenses.
* Assess your liquidity, solvency, and overall financial stability.

3. Product/Service Evaluation:

* Evaluate the performance of your products or services in the market.
* Gather feedback from customers regarding product quality, features, pricing, and customer service.
* Identify any areas for improvement or innovation to enhance your offerings.

4. Customer Analysis:

* Understand your customer demographics, behaviors, and preferences.
* Analyze customer feedback, reviews, and satisfaction levels.
* Assess customer retention rates and lifetime value.

5. Operational Efficiency:

* Review your operational processes, supply chain, and logistics.
* Identify any inefficiencies or bottlenecks that may be impacting productivity or cost-effectiveness.
* Explore opportunities for streamlining operations and improving efficiency.

6. Brand Perception:

* Evaluate the perception of your brand among customers and in the market.
* Assess brand awareness, reputation, and loyalty.
* Identify strengths to leverage and areas for brand enhancement.

7. SWOT Analysis:

* Conduct a SWOT (Strengths, Weaknesses, Opportunities, Threats) analysis to summarize key findings and insights.
* Identify strategic priorities and areas for focus based on the SWOT analysis.

By thoroughly assessing these aspects, you'll develop a clear understanding of where your business stands today and be better equipped to make informed decisions and strategic plans for future growth and success.

B. What I Think of My Business?

What you think of your business is a reflection of your perception, beliefs, and aspirations regarding its current state and future potential. Your thoughts about your business can influence your attitude, decision-making, and actions. Here are some aspects to consider in understanding what you think of your business:

1. Vision and Mission:
* Reflect on the overarching purpose and goals of your business.
* Consider whether you believe in the mission and vision you've set for your business and if you see them as achievable.

2. Strengths and Weaknesses:
 * Assess the strengths and weaknesses of your business from your perspective.
* Identify areas where you believe your business excels and areas where there is room for improvement.

3. Value Proposition:
* Consider how you perceive the value proposition of your business.
* Evaluate whether you believe your products or services effectively address customer needs and provide unique benefits.

4. Brand Identity:
* Reflect on how you view your business's brand identity and reputation.
* Consider whether you believe your brand effectively communicates its values, personality, and differentiation.

5. Growth Potential:
* Evaluate your confidence in the growth potential of your business.
* Consider factors such as market opportunities, competitive advantages, and scalability.

6. Challenges and Opportunities:
* Assess your perception of the challenges and opportunities facing your business.
* Identify obstacles that you believe need to be overcome and opportunities that you want to capitalise on.

7. Emotional Connection:
* Consider the emotional connection you have with your business.
* Reflect on your passion, commitment, and sense of fulfillment derived from running your business.

By examining your thoughts about your business across these dimensions, you can gain clarity on your overall perspective and mindset. This understanding can inform strategic planning, decision-making, and actions aimed at nurturing and growing your business.

C. What I think of myself?

Understanding what you think of yourself is essential for personal growth and development. Your self-perception influences your beliefs, behaviours, and interactions with others. Here are some aspects to consider in exploring what you think of yourself:

1. Self-Identity:
   * Reflect on how you define yourself and your identity.
   * Consider your values, beliefs, interests, and personality traits that shape your sense of self.

2. Self-Worth:
   * Evaluate your feelings of self-worth and self-esteem.
   * Consider whether you view yourself positively, recognizing your strengths and accomplishments, or if you struggle with self-doubt and insecurities.

3. Self-Image:
   * Reflect on how you perceive your physical appearance and body image.
   * Consider whether you feel confident and comfortable in your own skin or if you experience negative feelings about your appearance.

4. Self-Reflection:
   * Assess your ability to self-reflect and introspect.
   * Consider whether you engage in self-awareness practices, such as mindfulness or journaling, to gain insights into your thoughts, emotions, and behaviors.

5. Self-Compassion:
   * Evaluate your level of self-compassion and self-acceptance.
   * Consider whether you are kind and understanding towards yourself, especially during times of difficulty or failure.

6. Self-Confidence:
 * Assess your self-confidence and belief in your abilities.
 * Consider whether you approach challenges with a sense of empowerment and resilience or if you struggle with self-doubt and fear of failure.

8. Self-Development:
 * Reflect on your commitment to personal growth and self-improvement.
 * Consider whether you actively seek opportunities for learning, growth, and skill development.

By exploring these aspects of self-perception, you can gain insight into how you view yourself and identify areas for personal growth and development. Cultivating a positive self-image and nurturing self-compassion can contribute to greater well-being and fulfillment in life.

D. Am I doing it right?

The question "Am I doing it right?" reflects a desire for self-assessment and self-validation regarding one's actions, decisions, and behavior. Here are some considerations to help you evaluate whether you believe you are on the right path:

1. Alignment with Values:
 * Reflect on whether your actions align with your core values and principles.
 * Consider whether you feel a sense of integrity and authenticity in your decisions and behaviors.

2. Impact on Others:
 * Evaluate the impact of your actions on others, including colleagues, friends, family, and the broader community.
 * Consider whether your actions contribute positively to the well-being and happiness of those around you.

3. Goal Progression:
 * Assess whether your actions are helping you progress towards your goals and aspirations.
 * Consider whether you feel a sense of fulfillment and accomplishment in the pursuit of your objectives.

4. Learning and Growth:
 * Reflect on whether you are open to feedback, learning, and self-improvement.

* Consider whether you view challenges and setbacks as opportunities for growth and development.

5. Intentionality:
 * Evaluate whether you are acting with intention and purpose, rather than reacting impulsively or passively.
 * Consider whether you are mindful of the consequences of your actions and the long-term impact they may have.

6. Emotional Well-being:
 * Reflect on whether your actions contribute to your emotional well-being and happiness.
 * Consider whether you feel a sense of peace, contentment, and fulfillment in your daily life.

7. Ethical Considerations:
 * Assess whether your actions are ethical and morally sound.
 * Consider whether you are upholding principles of honesty, fairness, and compassion in your interactions with others.

By considering these aspects, you can gain clarity on whether you believe you are making the right choices and living in alignment with your values and aspirations.

MRI Brain - How to draw a Brain map

Let's start the MRI Brain exercise by creating a brain map to explore your thoughts and perceptions about the principles learned from management and self-help books. Remember that self-assessment is an ongoing process, and it's okay to reassess and adjust your course as needed to continue growing and evolving.

Can I see inside my brain? Brain maps will give us an exact scan of how we think about the subject.

Certainly! Here's how we can create a simple Brain map to represent various types of thoughts that come to mind when thinking about a specific subject:

Take an A4-sized blank white paper. do not use ruled or lined paper

1. Choose a Subject:
Select a subject you'd like to explore through a visual representation of a
Brain map. It could be a personal goal, a project, a relationship, or any other
topic of interest. The brain map describes how you think of the subject,
person, or objective inside your brain. You may mention your name, your
business name, your investment name, or the project name inside the
circle. You may even choose to mentionthe names of loved ones, partners,
or specific objectives.

2. Draw a Circle at the center:
Start by drawing a large circle with freehand in the center of your blank
paper. This circle represents your mind or consciousness. Do not use a scale
or a protractor to draw any line, circle, or oval.

3. Write the Subject Inside the Circle:
Write the name of the chosen subject inside the circle. This serves as the
focal point of your thoughts.

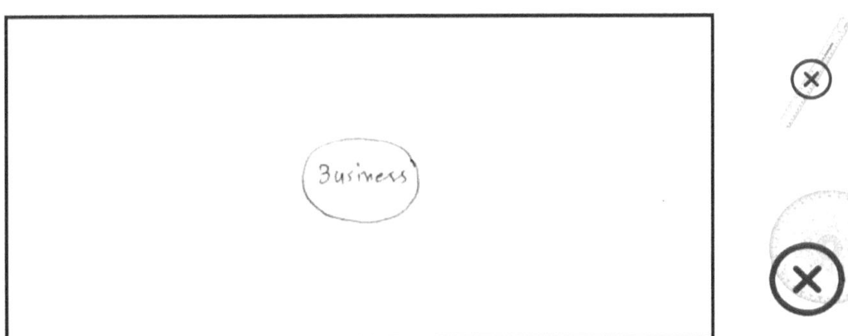

4. Draw Thought Bubbles:
The second step is to draw another circle or oval freehand in the blank
space and write the first thought that comes to your mind. Do not use a
scale or protector to draw circles. Around the center circle, draw several
smaller circles or cloud shapes to represent thought bubbles. These
thought bubbles will contain the different types of thoughts that come to
your mind about the subject. Continue this process, adding more circles or
ovals branching out from the central circle, each representing a different
thought or reflection related to your perception of these principles.

5. Write Thoughts Inside the Bubbles: Inside each thought bubble, write down a specific thought or idea that comes to your mind when thinking about the subject. These thoughts can be positive, negative, creative, practical, or any other type of thoughts that might arise.

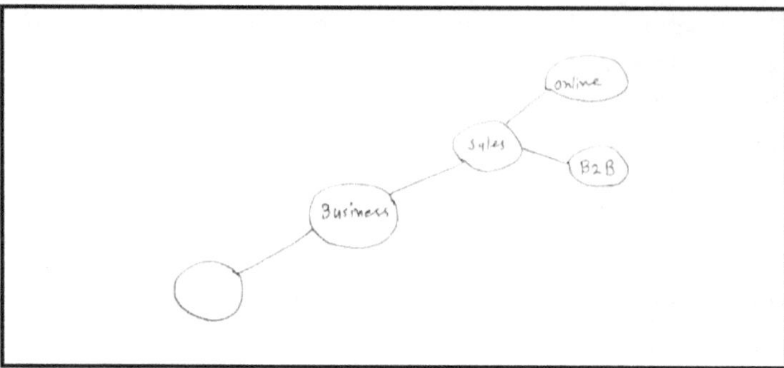

Image Brain map center circle with thought bubbles

6. Connect the Thoughts: Draw lines or arrows connecting related thoughts. This will help illustrate the connections and associations between different ideas.

7. Add Secondary thoughts Details: You can add a circle next to your second circle to further illustrate the nature of each thought. Repeat the same activity for every next thought that comes to your mind. You have completed the second layer of thoughts that come to your mind about the subject.

8. Reflect: Take a moment to reflect on the completed drawing and consider the insights that it has provided into your thought process about the chosen subject. Be honest and open with yourself as you explore your thoughts on the subject.

Once you've completed the Brain map drawing, you'll have a visual representation of the various thoughts and ideas associated with the subject, providing valuable insights into your perception and understanding. You'll gain valuable insights into how you perceive and engage with the principles you've learned, providing a clearer understanding of your mindset and potential areas for growth.

Let's begin the Analysis!

Absolutely, analyzing before drawing a new brain map is a wise approach, as it allows for reflection and deeper understanding of how thoughts evolve over time. Each iteration of the brain map captures a snapshot of your thoughts at a particular moment, offering valuable insights into your evolving perspective and learning journey.

Image Brain map centre circle with multi layer thought bubbles

Here's a suggested process for analyzing brain map:

1. Reflection: Take some time to reflect on your current thoughts and perceptions about the subject you want to explore.

2. Analysis: Consider the key questions, challenges, or areas of interest related to the subject. Analyze your thoughts and feelings about these aspects.

3. Brain Map Creation: Based on your analysis, create a brain map to visually represent your current thoughts. Follow the steps outlined earlier to draw the brain map on paper.

4. Review and Reflect: Once the brain map is complete, review it carefully. Reflect on the patterns, connections, and insights revealed by the map.

5. Identify Learnings: Identify any new learnings or insights gained from the analysis of the brain map. Consider how your understanding of the subject has evolved since the previous brain map.

6. Repeat Process: As thoughts evolve and new learnings emerge, repeat the process of reflection, analysis, brain map creation, and review. Each iteration will contribute to a deeper understanding of the subject and your own thought processes.

By following this iterative approach, you will continually uncover new insights and perspectives, enriching your learning journey and enhancing your ability to navigate complex subjects. Remember that the goal is not perfection, but rather continuous growth and learning.

How to Review and reflect on thoughts within the Brain map

The key to success lies in the quality of analysis and the insights gained from examining the brain map, rather than the artistic perfection of the drawing itself. Here are a few reasons why:

1. Insight Generation: The primary purpose of creating a brain map is to gain insights into your thoughts, perceptions, and understanding of a particular subject. The process of analyzing the brain map allows you to uncover patterns, connections, and areas for further exploration.

2. Self-Reflection: By analyzing the brain map, you engage in a process of self-reflection and introspection. You gain a deeper understanding of your own thought processes, biases, and areas of strength and weakness.

3. Decision Making: The insights gained from analyzing the brain map can inform decision-making and problem-solving. You can identify opportunities for improvement, areas where additional research or action is needed, and strategies for achieving your goals.

4. Continuous Learning: Analyzing brain maps on a regular basis facilitates continuous learning and personal growth. As you reflect on your thoughts and experiences over time, you gain new insights and perspectives that contribute to your development.

5. Adaptability: A good analysis of the brain map enables you to adapt and adjust your approach as needed. You can identify changes in your thinking, external factors influencing the subject, and new opportunities or challenges that arise.

In summary, while the process of drawing a brain map is important for plotting your thoughts, it is the diagnosis of the thoughts that ultimately leads to success. By focusing on thoughtful analysis and reflection, you can unlock valuable insights that contribute to your personal and professional growth.

Here are the key findings that we will be discussing in the next chapters:

- Brain map exercise with the sales head of the Multi-National Company (Profit first maintaining top-line growth)
- Brain map exercise with the founder of a listed company (Shareholder's wealth)
- Brain map exercise with the shopkeeper (Personal growth)
- Brain map exercise with Exporter (Strategic Exploration)
- Brain map exercise with Builder (Customer insight - Sales Potential)
- Brain map exercise with Columnist (Self-discovery)
- Brain map exercise with the retail shop owner (employee retention)
- Brain map exercise about loved ones (Relationship)
- Brain map exercise about myself (happiness & spirituality)

Chapter 2: How to Develop Your Power Center

Once identified, these power centers require nurturing and cultivation. This chapter delves into practical strategies for harnessing our strengths and channeling them toward growth and success.

In the previous chapter, we learned how to draw a Brain map. In this chapter, we are going to learn about the analysis of the brain map.

Diagnosis: First Layer Thoughts

In the realm of brain mapping, the initial layer of thoughts serves as the cornerstone upon which deeper insights are built. This section delves into the significance of first-layer thoughts and their role in shaping our understanding of a subject.

When we embark on the journey of creating a brain map, the first layer of thoughts emerges effortlessly. Like clockwork, the initial thought bubbles form, next to the central circle, representing our immediate perceptions and opinions about the subject at hand.

Contemplating Actions: What do we want to do?

In the intricate complex of the human mind, thoughts are the silent architects of our reality, shaping our perceptions and steering our actions. Among these, first-layer thoughts hold a special place – they are the immediate, often emotional responses that emerge in the vessel of our consciousness. It is here, amidst the crowded marketplace of ideas, that we find people engaging in the timeless dance of introspection and expression.

At the forefront of the first-layer thoughts lies the perpetual inquiry into desire and intention. What do we want to do? This simple yet profound question serves as the compass guiding our endeavors and as the North Star illuminating the path ahead. From the boring to the elevated, our aspirations flicker like candle flames in the dark recesses of our minds, casting shadows that hint at the contours of our innermost desires.

For some, first-layer thoughts are a fabric woven with threads of ambition and aspiration. They envision grand schemes and lofty goals, their minds ablaze with the intensity of possibility. With each thought, they sketch the blueprint of their dreams, painting vibrant strokes on the canvas of their imagination.

Whether scaling the heights of professional success or charting the uncharted territories of personal growth, they are driven by an insatiable hunger for more – more knowledge, more experiences, more life.

Yet, first-layer thoughts are not always a symphony of triumph and ambition. They can also be a battleground where doubts and insecurities clash in fierce combat. Beneath the veneer of confidence and certainty lie the whispers of fear and uncertainty, gnawing away at the edges of our resolve. What if we fail? What if we're not good enough? These questions lurk in the shadows, casting a pall over our aspirations and sowing seeds of doubt in the fertile soil of our minds.

And then there are those whose first layer of thoughts is a mosaic of conflicting desires and competing priorities. They navigate the complex of their minds with the skill of seasoned cartographers, tracing the intricate pathways that lead to divergent destinations. Caught between duty and desire, obligation and passion, they wrestle with the paradox of choice, seeking elusive equilibrium in a world of endless possibilities.

But amidst the noise of first-layer thoughts, there is a common thread that binds us all – the innate human desire for meaning and purpose. Whether we articulate it in the language of ambition or insecurity, certainty or doubt, our thoughts are but echoes of the fundamental quest to find our place in the vast varieties of existence.

In the realm of first-layer thoughts, we are both architects and artisans, sculpting the contours of our reality with each fleeting thought. It is a realm of infinite possibility and boundless potential, where the only limit is the scope of our imagination. And as we journey deeper into the recesses of our minds, may we continue to explore the complex of our thoughts with courage, curiosity, and an unwavering belief in the power of our dreams.

Reflecting on Possession: What we possess?

In the varieties of human consciousness, thoughts about possessions weave a rich and complex narrative, reflecting our relationship with the material world that surrounds us. From the tangible to the intangible, from the boring to the extraordinary, our possessions serve as both mirrors and milestones, shaping our identities and influencing our perceptions.
At the heart of thoughts about what we have lies a profound meditation on abundance and scarcity.

Whether we possess great wealth or modest means, our possessions are a lens through which we view ourselves and our place in the world. They are the tangible manifestations of our endeavors, the fruits of our labor, and the artifacts of our existence.

For some, thoughts about possessions are a source of pride and accomplishment, a testament to their hard work and perseverance. They revel in the tangible evidence of their success – the shining trophies of their achievements, the luxurious trappings of their lifestyle. Each possession is a badge of honor, a symbol of their prowess in the arena of life.

Yet, for others, thoughts about possessions are tinged with a sense of longing and inadequacy. They gaze upon the possessions of others with envy and yearning, measuring their own worth against the yardstick of material wealth. Caught in the relentless pursuit of more and more money, status, and trappings, they find themselves trapped in a cycle of consumption. They seek solace in the fleeting pleasures of acquisition.

And then there are those whose thoughts about possessions are spread over with gratitude and contentment. They find joy not in the accumulation of things, but in the simple abundance of everyday life, the warmth of a loving relationship, the beauty of a sunset, the laughter of a child. To them, possessions are but fleeting shadows, transitory reminders of the transient nature of existence.

But amidst the ebb and flow of thoughts about possessions, there is a deeper truth that goes beyond the material empire. The realization that true wealth lies not in what we have, but in who we are. It is a wealth measured not in bank balances or possessions, but in the richness of our experiences, the depth of our relationships, and the resilience of our spirit.

In the realm of thoughts about possessions, we are both collectors and curators, guardians of the treasures that populate the landscape of our lives. May we approach our possessions with mindfulness and gratitude, recognizing their transient nature, and may we embrace the abundance that surrounds us in every moment. And as we journey through life, may we remember that the most precious possessions are those that reside not in our hands, but in our hearts.

Aspirations Unveiled: What do we want to be?

In the realm of self-reflection, thoughts about what we want to be are like unfiltered streams, flowing freely from the depths of our consciousness. Here, amidst the raw honesty of our innermost desires, we lay bare our aspirations and ambitions, casting aside the veil of social convention to reveal the true essence of our being.

At the heart of thoughts about what we want to be, lies a bold declaration of identity and purpose. They are the clarion call of our innermost selves, signaling us towards paths that resonate with our deepest values and passions. Whether it's envisioning ourselves as leaders in our chosen field, innovators in uncharted territory, or simply as individuals who make a positive impact on the world, these thoughts are the compass that guides us toward our true north.

For some, thoughts about what they want to be are a testament to their unconstrained ambition and drive. They see themselves as captains of industry, entrepreneurs who dare to defy convention and carve out their own destiny. Business, to them, is not just a means to an end, but a canvas on which they paint their grandest visions, leaving an indelible mark on the world with each stroke of their ambition.

Yet, for others, thoughts about what they want to be are tempered by a sense of pragmatism and realism. They understand that success is not guaranteed and that the road to achievement is paved with challenges and setbacks. And yet, they refuse to be deterred by the odds, seeing every obstacle as an opportunity to learn and grow. To them, business is not just about profits and bottom lines, but about building meaningful connections, fostering collaboration, and creating value that extends far beyond the balance sheet.

And then there are those whose thoughts about what they want to be are guided by a deep sense of purpose and meaning. They see themselves not as titans of industry or captains of commerce, but as stewards of a greater good. To them, business is not just about making money, but about making a difference – in the lives of their employees, in the communities they serve, and in the world at large. They aspire not to be the biggest or the wealthiest, but to be the best – not just for themselves, but for the greater good of humanity.

But amidst the diversity of thoughts about what we want to be, there is a common thread that binds us all – the desire to lead lives of purpose and fulfillment, to be true to ourselves, and to make a positive impact on the world around us. Whether we articulate it in the language of ambition or altruism, pragmatism or passion, our thoughts are but echoes of the fundamental human quest to find meaning and fulfillment in our lives.

In the realm of thoughts about what we want to be, we are both dreamers and doers, visionaries who dare to imagine a better world, and architects who roll up their sleeves and get to work to make that vision a reality. May we approach each thought with courage and conviction, embracing the journey of self-discovery with open hearts and open minds. And as we navigate the complexities of our inner landscape, may we find solace in the knowledge that the true measure of success lies not in what we achieve, but in who we become along the way.

It's fascinating to note that these first-layer thoughts often revolve around fundamental aspects such as desires, possessions, and aspirations. Individuals readily express thoughts about what they want to do, what they have, and what they want to be. There is a sense of openness and transparency in these initial reflections, as individuals lay bare their opinions without hesitation.

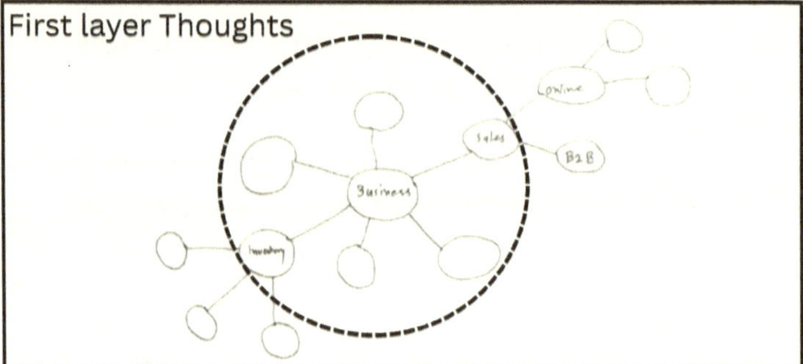

These top-of-the-mind thoughts provide valuable insights into how individuals perceive the subject, whether it's a business venture, a department within an organization, or a personal goal. By examining these initial impressions, we can gain a clear understanding of their perspective and mindset.

It's intriguing to observe that individuals tend to allocate a significant portion of their view of the subject to the first layer of thoughts—approximately 30 to 35 percent. This allocation reflects their confidence and expertise in the subject matter, showcasing their mastery through experience or professional qualifications. Armed with this depth of knowledge, individuals possess the ability to influence others and shape perceptions with their clarity of thought.

However, the true essence of growth hacking lies beyond the surface-level perceptions captured in the first layer of thoughts. As the chapter aptly highlights, growth hacking involves delving into the second and third layers of thoughts, akin to advancing from a degree certificate to a master's degree and finally to a doctorate research degree.

Achieving clarity at these deeper layers requires a willingness to explore beyond the obvious, challenge assumptions, and engage in critical analysis. It is through this process of exploration and refinement that individuals uncover new insights, identify innovative solutions, and drive meaningful progress in their endeavors.

In essence, while first-layer thoughts provide a solid foundation, it is the journey into the deeper layers that unlocks the true potential for growth and innovation. As we continue to explore the intricacies of brain mapping, let us not underestimate the power of delving beyond the surface and embracing the complexity of thought.

Diagnosis: Second Layer Thoughts

In the journey of brain mapping, the exploration of second layer thoughts presents unique challenges and insights. This section examines the complexities and observations associated with second layer thoughts, shedding light on their significance and impact.

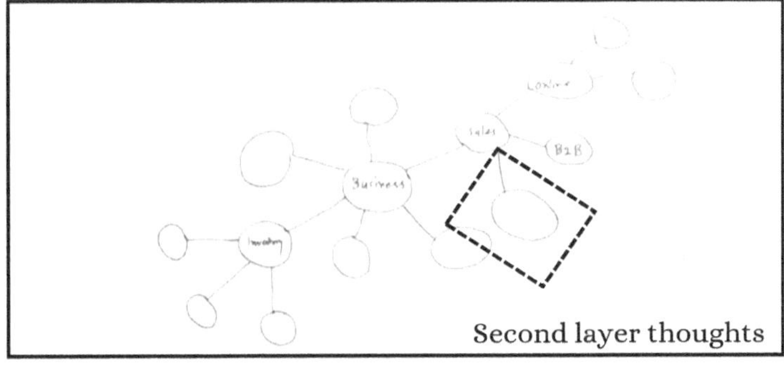

Second layer thoughts

Observation One:
Many individuals encounter difficulties when attempting to draw second-layer thoughts, often attributed to space constraints on an A4 size sheet. This reluctance to delve deeper into the second layer may stem from several factors:

- **Perceived Insignificance**: Some individuals may not consider second-layer thoughts significant enough to warrant immediate attention.
- **Overconfidence**: Others may believe they can easily address these thoughts later, underestimating their importance.
- **Lack of Depth**: Individuals may lack a thorough understanding or practical experience in the area represented by the second-layer of thoughts.

This reluctance to address second-layer thoughts does not necessarily indicate carelessness but rather a sense of confidence in one's ability to handle them when the time comes.

Observation Two:
Another observation regarding second-layer thoughts is the tendency for thought bubbles to be connected by perpendicular lines or inward angles of less than 90 degrees. These inward connections often signify weak or off-tangent thoughts that require further exploration and refinement.

Individuals may struggle with clarity or depth in these thoughts, often experiencing them on the spur of the moment without a solid foundation. To address this, it's crucial to gain clarity and depth in execution, considering key parameters discussed in earlier chapters.

An example illustrates this point vividly: a sales head of The Hague based MNC expressed a desire to explore new markets to increase revenue. However, upon examining his brain map, it became evident that his second-layer thoughts regarding new markets were connected inwardly, indicating a lack of knowledge or fear of market acceptance. Through guidance and market research, he gained clarity, enabling him to take calculated risks and expand successfully into new markets.

Observation Three:
In some instances, second-layer thoughts may overlap neighboring thoughts, indicating a strong connection between them. This overlap suggests a dependency, relative theory, or sequential approach between the thoughts, highlighting the need for clarity and understanding.

For instance, a shopkeeper lamented his inability to increase sales due to a lack of funds for stocking inventory. However, upon closer examination of his brain map, it was evident that his thoughts on money overlapped with those on sales, reflecting a financial illiteracy. Through education on budgeting and investment, he gained clarity, allowing him to manage expenses effectively and grow his business exponentially.

In conclusion, while second-layer thoughts pose challenges, they also present opportunities for growth and clarity. By addressing these observations and working towards greater depth and understanding, individuals can unlock new avenues for success and innovation in their endeavors.

Diagnosis: Third Layer Thoughts

Exploring the depths of brain mapping reveals the intricacies of third-layer thoughts, which are characterized by action-oriented strategies and tactics. This section delves into the nature of third-layer thoughts, highlighting their significance and the observations associated with them.
Understanding Third Layer Thoughts:

Third-layer thoughts are distinguished by their focus on action and tactics. Individuals who delve into this layer are often skilled in their respective areas and possess a deep understanding of how to execute tasks effectively. They derive satisfaction from the execution process and devote significant time to mastering their craft.

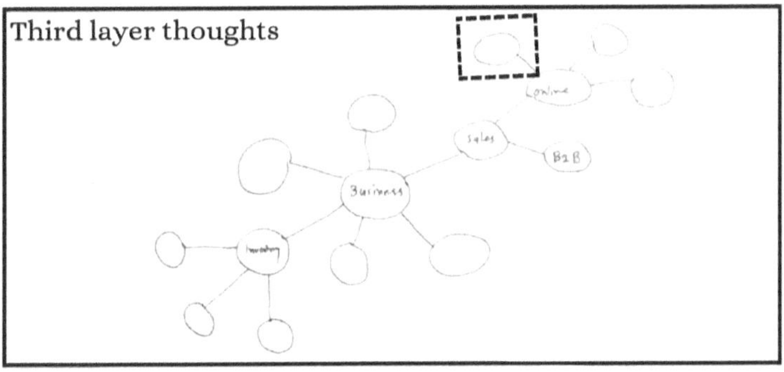

Despite their proficiency, individuals may not always share their third layer thoughts as they perceive them to be their core strength. Instead, they prefer to let their actions speak for themselves, quietly driving progress and achieving results.

Observations and Remedies:
Similar observations may be made regarding third-layer thoughts as discussed earlier for second-layer thoughts. For instance, individuals may struggle with clarity or depth in their third-layer thoughts, leading to challenges in execution. The remedies for addressing these challenges remain consistent: gaining clarity, exploring alternative perspectives, and refining strategies.

Overall Brain Map Interpretations:
An interesting observation when examining brain maps with third-layer thoughts is the presence of plant-like branches connecting various thoughts. These branches signify clarity of thought and a progressive mindset. Individuals with such brain maps demonstrate a holistic understanding of the subject and possess the ability to navigate complex challenges with ease.

It's essential to recognize that no matter how skilled individuals are in their respective areas, they can always benefit from assembling a team with complementary skill sets. This collaborative approach ensures comprehensive coverage of all aspects of the subject and enhances the likelihood of growth.

An illustrative example of this concept is evident in the experience of a CEO friend with financial skills leading engineering companies. Despite lacking expertise in engineering products, their brain map focuses on business strategies rather than technical details. This strategic approach underscores the importance of leveraging individual strengths while assembling a diverse team to drive organizational growth.

In conclusion, thoughts represent the culmination of expertise and action-oriented strategies. By embracing clarity of thought and fostering a progressive mindset, individuals can navigate challenges effectively and achieve growth hacking.

Indeed, the beauty of brain mapping lies in its universal applicability across businesses of all sizes and various aspects of life, including relationships. Whether you're a small shopkeeper or the head of a multi-billion-dollar corporation, brain mapping serves as a powerful tool for identifying thought blockages and unlocking pathways to growth hacking.

By examining the intricate web of thoughts and perceptions represented in a brain map, individuals can pinpoint areas where they may be experiencing challenges or limitations. Whether it's in business strategy, marketing tactics, operational efficiency, or interpersonal dynamics, the insights gleaned from a thorough analysis of the brain map can pave the way for transformative change and innovation.

Moreover, the process of brain mapping isn't limited to business contexts alone. It can also be applied to resurrecting personal relationships, helping individuals understand the dynamics at play, identify areas for improvement, and foster greater understanding and harmony.

Through observation and analysis, individuals can witness the remarkable transformation that occurs as thought blockages are identified and addressed. From small businesses experiencing exponential growth to established corporations navigating complex challenges, the power of brain mapping knows no bounds.

The journey of growth hacking is as much about introspection and self-discovery as it is about external strategies and tactics. By harnessing the insights provided by brain mapping, individuals can unlock their full potential and achieve unprecedented success in both business and personal spheres.

Unveiling Thought Blockages for Growth Hacking

In the ever-evolving landscape of business, the journey to growth and success is often hindered by unseen barriers lurking within the depths of our minds. Like hidden reefs beneath the surface of calm waters, these thought blockages can impede progress and stifle innovation, casting a shadow over even the most promising ventures. Yet, with the aid of a powerful tool known as the brain map, entrepreneurs of all stripes – from small-time shopkeepers to captains of industry overseeing billion-dollar enterprises – can uncover and overcome these obstacles, unlocking the full potential of their businesses and resurrecting relationships with newfound clarity and purpose.

At the heart of the brain map lies a simple yet profound insight: that the key to unlocking growth lies not in external factors or market conditions, but in the inner workings of the human mind. By charting the intricate pathways of thought and emotion that shape our perceptions and behaviors, entrepreneurs can gain invaluable insights into the underlying drivers of their business success – or lack thereof.

For some, the journey begins with a humble corner shop, where the proprietor grapples with the age-old challenge of attracting and retaining customers in a fiercely competitive marketplace.
Through the lens of the brain map, they uncover hidden biases and limiting beliefs that have long hindered their ability to innovate and adapt. With newfound clarity, they embark on a journey of self-discovery, transforming their shop into a thriving hub of community activity, where customers are not just patrons, but cherished members of an extended family.

Yet, the power of the brain map is not limited to small-scale enterprises – far from it. Even the most formidable business behemoths can benefit from its insights, as they seek to navigate the complexities of an ever-changing global economy.
For CEOs and executives overseeing billion-dollar enterprises, the brain map offers a unique vantage point from which to identify and address the hidden barriers to growth that lurk within their organisations.
Whether it's entrenched bureaucracies stifling innovation or outdated modes of thinking impeding progress, the brain map serves as a powerful tool for dismantling the status quo and ushering in a new era of growth and prosperity.

And then there are those who have mastered the art of resurrecting relationships – not just between businesses and their customers, but between individuals and the communities they serve.
Through the lens of the brain map, they uncover the hidden dynamics of human interaction that underpin successful relationships, from trust and empathy to communication and collaboration.
Armed with this knowledge, they forge connections that transcend mere transactions, building bridges of understanding and goodwill that endure long after the sale is made.

But perhaps the greatest gift of the brain map lies not in its ability to uncover hidden barriers or resurrect relationships, but in its capacity to awaken the dormant potential that lies within each of us. By shining a light on the hidden recesses of our minds, it empowers us to break free from the shackles of limiting beliefs and self-imposed constraints, unleashing a tidal wave of creativity, innovation, and growth.

In the realm of business, no challenge is too daunting, no obstacle too insurmountable for those armed with the power of the brain map. Whether you're a small-time shopkeeper or a corporate titan, its insights offer a roadmap to success, guiding you on a journey of self-discovery and transformation.

So, as you embark on the adventure of entrepreneurship, remember that the greatest opportunities for growth lie not in the external world, but within the boundless reaches of your own mind.

Developing Your Power Center Through Brain Mapping

In today's fast-paced world, mastering the art of personal development is essential for success. One powerful approach to self-improvement is through understanding and harnessing the potential of your brain. In this chapter, we will explore the concept of developing your power center by utilizing brain mapping techniques. By the end, you'll have a clear roadmap to unlock your true potential and achieve your goals.

Understanding Brain Mapping:

Brain mapping is a method used to visualize the structure and function of the brain. Through advanced technologies such as functional magnetic resonance imaging (fMRI) and electroencephalography (EEG), scientists can map different regions of the brain responsible for various functions and behaviors. This information is invaluable for understanding how our brains work and how we can optimize them for peak performance.

Identifying Your Power Center:

Your power center refers to the core aspects of yourself that drive your thoughts, emotions, and actions. By identifying your strengths, weaknesses, passions, and values, you can pinpoint your power center and leverage it to achieve your goals. Brain mapping can help you uncover these key areas by revealing patterns in your brain activity associated with different cognitive functions.

Steps to Develop Your Power Center:

- **Self-Reflection:** Begin by reflecting on your past experiences, successes, and challenges. What activities energize you? What tasks do you excel at? Understanding your strengths and weaknesses is the first step towards developing your power center.
- **Brain Mapping:** Consult with a professional who specializes in brain mapping or use online tools to conduct a self-assessment. These tools analyze your brain activity patterns to identify areas of strength and areas that may need improvement.
- **Set Clear Goals:** Based on the insights gained from your brain mapping analysis, set clear and achievable goals that align with your power center. Whether it's advancing in your career, improving relationships, or enhancing your overall well-being, define what success looks like for you.

- **Mindfulness Practices:** Incorporate mindfulness practices such as meditation, deep breathing exercises, or visualization techniques into your daily routine. These practices help calm the mind, reduce stress, and improve focus, allowing you to tap into your power center more effectively.
- **Continuous Learning:** Never stop learning and growing. Take advantage of opportunities to expand your knowledge and skills in areas that align with your power center. Whether it's through formal education, online courses, or self-directed study, investing in your personal development is key to unlocking your full potential.
- **Feedback and Adaptation:** Seek feedback from mentors, peers, or coaches to gain valuable insights into your progress. Be open to constructive criticism and willing to adapt your approach as needed. Remember, personal development is an ongoing journey of self-discovery and improvement.

Developing your power center through brain mapping is a transformative journey that empowers you to reach new heights of success and fulfillment. By understanding your brain's unique wiring and leveraging your strengths, you can overcome obstacles, achieve your goals, and live a life of purpose and passion. Embrace the process, stay committed to your growth, and watch as your power center becomes the driving force behind your success.

Mastering Your Growth Thought Through Brain Mapping Layers

In the journey of personal development, understanding the layers of your thoughts and how they intersect is crucial for maximizing your growth potential. In this chapter, we will delve into the process of identifying and optimizing your thought layers using brain mapping techniques. By focusing your efforts on the right areas and simplifying complex thoughts, you can achieve exponential growth and clarity of mind.

1. Identifying Your Thought Layers:
Begin by mapping out your thoughts on paper, starting from the surface level (Layer 1) to deeper levels of complexity (Layer 3). The top right corner of the page typically represents your first layer of clear, focused thoughts. This is where you should allocate the majority of your efforts, as these thoughts are well-defined and easy to act upon.

2. Simplifying Complex Thoughts:

As you delve deeper into your thought layers, pay attention to any overlapping or intersecting thoughts between Layer 2 and Layer 3. These areas indicate complexity and may require simplification for optimal growth. Focus on untangling these thoughts by breaking them down into smaller, more manageable components. By simplifying complex thoughts, you create room for exponential growth and clearer decision-making.

3. Strengthening Low-Stake Afterthoughts:

Identify any areas on your brain map where you've drawn reverse thoughts or thought lines at right angles. These low-stake afterthoughts often represent less critical aspects of your thinking process. Strengthen these areas by reinforcing positive thought patterns and reinforcing your core beliefs. While these thoughts may seem less significant, they contribute to overall mental resilience and well-being.

4. Leveraging Bank Space for Learning:

If you find that you've left blank space on your brain map, consider it an opportunity for exploration and learning. Blank space indicates room for growth and new ideas. Use this space to brainstorm, experiment with new concepts, and expand your horizons. Embrace the unknown and allow yourself the freedom to play and learn without constraints.

5. Taking Breaks and Redrawing Your Brain Map:

Finally, recognize the importance of taking breaks to recharge and reflect on your learnings. After a period of intense focus, step away from your brain map and give yourself time to rest and rejuvenate. Use this break time to internalize your insights and allow them to sink in. After a few hours, return to your brain map with fresh eyes and corrections. Redraw any areas that need adjustment and continue refining your thought layers.

Mastering your growth thought layers through brain mapping is a dynamic process that requires self-awareness, patience, and perseverance. By identifying clear thoughts, simplifying complexity, strengthening low-stake afterthoughts, and leveraging blank space for learning, you can unlock your full potential and achieve greater clarity of mind. Remember to take breaks, reflect on your progress, and embrace the journey of self-discovery and growth.

Chapter 3: Be Rough but Kind at Heart

In navigating life's challenges, it's crucial to strike a delicate balance between assertiveness and compassion. This chapter delves into the art of being firm in our pursuits while maintaining empathy for others.

Often, we witness supervisors who resort to yelling at their team members for their mistakes. Surprisingly, despite the harshness, they can foster long-lasting relationships with their coworkers. It's akin to the dynamic between an army major and their soldiers; despite the authoritative commands, there's a deep-seated camaraderie that endures. Humans possess an innate ability to perceive love beyond mere words.

Take, for instance, my perfectionist friend who serves as the Production head of a large organization. He's constantly under pressure to meet targets and uphold a zero-defect product strategy. While he may falter in his communication at times, he compensates by intricately understanding the personal needs of his coworkers. He goes above and beyond to nurture relationships, knowing hundreds of workers' children's names, their educational milestones, and even details about their personal lives. His capacity for empathy shines through despite his demanding role.

Similarly, I have a friend who is a shopkeeper in London, known for his demeanor with regular customers. However, it was observed that behind the rough exterior lay a heart of gold. He intuitively understands their needs and consistently goes out of his way to assist them, both socially and personally.

In a poignant example, a woman approached me with concerns about her abusive husband, at a lecture in New Delhi.

When asked why she hadn't sought divorce, she revealed a surprising truth. Despite his flaws, she acknowledged his underlying love for her but lamented his inability to control his temper and abusive language. Brain mapped through introspection, she realized her role in perpetuating certain triggers for his anger. By addressing these underlying issues and fostering open communication, they began to rebuild a happier, healthier relationship.

In essence, being rough around the edges doesn't negate the kindness within.

It's about recognizing our imperfections while striving to cultivate understanding, empathy, and love in our interactions with others.

In life, we often encounter situations where toughness is necessary to navigate challenges effectively. Whether it's setting boundaries, delivering constructive criticism, or pushing ourselves to achieve our goals, a certain level of assertiveness is required. However, amidst the rough exterior, it's imperative to cultivate kindness at the core.

Being rough but kind at heart is about finding the balance between strength and compassion. It's about recognizing that firmness doesn't have to equate to harshness and that empathy doesn't signify weakness. In fact, it's the ability to blend these seemingly contrasting qualities that enables us to connect with others on a deeper level.

When we're rough but kind at heart, we're able to assert ourselves confidently while remaining sensitive to the feelings and needs of those around us. We understand that being firm doesn't mean being callous and that being compassionate doesn't mean being a pushover. Instead, it means approaching each situation with integrity, honesty, and genuine concern for the well-being of others.

This approach is especially crucial in leadership roles, where effective communication and understanding are paramount. A leader who is rough but kind at heart commands respect through their decisiveness and strength, yet fosters loyalty and trust through their empathy and support. In personal relationships, being rough but kind at heart allows us to navigate conflicts with grace and understanding. It means speaking our truth with clarity and conviction, while also listening with an open mind and a compassionate heart.

Ultimately, being rough but kind at heart is a mindset—a commitment to upholding our principles with unwavering resolve, yet always tempering our actions with kindness, empathy, and love. It's a reminder that strength and compassion are not mutually exclusive, but rather, complementary forces that enable us to navigate life's complexities with grace and integrity.

Understanding and Managing Anger
Anger, a powerful and often overwhelming emotion, can have profound effects on both individuals and their surroundings.

In this chapter, we explore the complexities of anger, its impact on personal growth, and strategies for effectively managing this potent emotion.

The Uncontrollable Outburst:

My friend struggles with controlling his anger, feeling as though it erupts uncontrollably and without warning. He may justify his anger as a means of correcting mistakes or ensuring that others understand the severity of their actions. However, this approach often leads to escalating tensions and strained relationships.

The Paralysis of Anger:

Anger has a profound effect on the mind, clouding judgment and impairing rational thought. When consumed by anger, individuals may find themselves unable to think clearly or make sound decisions. This mental paralysis hinders personal growth and impedes progress towards achieving goals.

Understanding the Anger Process:

Anger typically manifests in stages, beginning with an initial trigger event or perceived wrongdoing. As individuals ruminate on the situation, they may interpret the actions of others in a negative light and choose to respond with anger. This process occurs within the intricate workings of the brain, highlighting the importance of managing one's thought processes to prevent anger from taking hold.

Harnessing Roughness without Anger:

An essential distinction to make is that one can express assertiveness and resolve without succumbing to anger. Like the surface of the sea, which may appear turbulent but remains calm in its depths, individuals can cultivate inner peace and composure even in the face of adversity. By mastering the art of anger management, individuals can navigate life's challenges with grace and resilience, tapping into the depths of their inner strength.

The Cost of Anger:

While anger may provide a temporary surge of energy and motivation, it often comes at a significant cost. By channeling all their focus and energy into their anger, individuals may neglect other critical aspects of their lives, hindering their overall growth and well-being. Additionally, while anger may enable individuals to win individual battles, it ultimately undermines their ability to achieve long-term success and growth.

In conclusion, understanding and managing anger is essential for personal growth and well-being. By recognizing the stages of anger and learning to control our responses, we can prevent this powerful emotion from hijacking our thoughts and actions. Instead of allowing anger to dictate our behavior, we can cultivate inner peace and resilience, harnessing our energy for productive endeavors and meaningful growth. In mastering the art of anger management, we unlock the path to greater self-awareness, emotional intelligence, and overall success in life.

Navigating Parental Expectations and Anger in Family Dynamics

In the intricate tapestry of family relationships, parental expectations and expressions of anger can profoundly influence the well-being and success of children. This chapter explores the challenges faced by a friend whose high expectations for his children are coupled with frequent outbursts of anger, and the transformative journey towards fostering a healthier family dynamic.

The Cycle of Anger and Discontent:
My protagonist friend, a father with lofty expectations for his children's academic and athletic achievements, finds himself trapped in a cycle of anger and discontent. Despite his deep understanding of finance, objectives, and his children's needs, his expressions of anger towards his family members sow seeds of discord and anxiety within the household.

Unraveling the Puzzle:
Upon examination of his brain map, it becomes evident that our protagonist's cluttered thoughts about his children's capabilities and execution hinder their growth and success. While he commands respect, his children also harbor a deep-seated fear of his anger, which permeates their academic and athletic endeavors. The children, consciously or subconsciously, may rebel against their father's expectations as a form of retaliation for his harsh demean.

Building Bridges through Understanding and Love:
Armed with this newfound insight through Brain map, my friend embarks on a journey of self-discovery and transformation. Rather than solely focusing on his children's academic and athletic achievements, he learns to prioritize building a loving and supportive family environment. By adopting a more compassionate and understanding approach, he aims to strengthen the bond with his children and cultivate a sense of trust and collaboration within the family unit.

Navigating the Path to Positive Change:
With guidance and support, my friend commits to becoming a more loving and approachable father figure. He invests time in reading books on anger management and team building, seeking to acquire the necessary skills to foster a healthier family dynamic.
Over time, his efforts yield tangible results, as his children begin to thrive academically and athletically, and happiness blossoms within the home.

The journey of my protagonist friend serves as a poignant reminder of the profound impact of parental expectations and expressions of anger on family dynamics. By recognizing the detrimental effects of his behavior and taking proactive steps towards positive change, he not only fosters a more supportive and loving environment for his children but also cultivates their growth and success. In navigating the complexities of parenthood, empathy, understanding, and love emerge as powerful catalysts for building strong and resilient family relationships.

Cultivating Inner Growth:
Nurturing Happiness and Positive Thought Patterns
In the journey of personal development, mastering the art of nurturing positivity and breaking free from negative thought patterns is crucial. It's a process that involves not only individual introspection but also nurturing healthy relationships and cultivating empathy towards others. Let's delve into the key steps towards this transformative journey:

Breaking Negative Thought Patterns
Negative thought patterns can be pervasive and damaging, affecting every aspect of our lives. However, recognizing and challenging these patterns is the first step towards liberation. Start by observing your thoughts without judgment. Identify recurring negative themes and challenge their validity. Replace them with positive affirmations and constructive thoughts. Practice gratitude daily to shift your focus towards the abundance in your life.

Stay Together, Pray Together, Grow Together
Strong relationships are built on a foundation of love, trust, and mutual support. By staying connected with your loved ones, sharing your joys and struggles, and nurturing a culture of open communication, you create a resilient bond that withstands challenges. Prayer, whether individually or as a couple/family, can provide solace, guidance, and a sense of connection to something greater than oneself. Together, you can grow emotionally, spiritually, and intellectually, strengthening the fabric of your relationships.

Choosing Happiness Thoughts

Happiness is not merely a result of external circumstances but a choice we make every day. Train your mind to focus on positive thoughts and moments of joy. Practice mindfulness to stay present and appreciate the beauty of each moment. Surround yourself with uplifting influences, whether it's uplifting books, inspiring music, or supportive friends. Remember, happiness is a journey, not a destination.

The Master Key: Being Happy While Developing Growth

Growth and happiness are intertwined. Embrace the process of growth hacking with enthusiasm and a positive mindset. Instead of viewing challenges as obstacles, see them as opportunities for growth and learning. Celebrate your progress, no matter how small, and cultivate a sense of fulfilment in every step of your journey. Remember, true success is not just achieving your goals but finding joy and contentment along the way.

Developing Happiness Within

True happiness comes from within. Cultivate practices that nourish your soul, such as meditation, journaling, or spending time in nature. Connect with your inner self and align your actions with your values and passions. Prioritize self-care and make time for activities that bring you joy. By nurturing your inner happiness, you radiate positivity and become a beacon of light for others.

Inner Speech Drives Growth

The way we talk to ourselves shapes our reality. Replace self-criticism with self-compassion and encouragement. Use affirmations to reprogram your subconscious mind and instill beliefs that empower you to reach your full potential. Practice positive self-talk consistently, especially during times of doubt or setbacks. Your inner speech can either fuel your growth or hinder it, so choose your words wisely.

Becoming Emotionally Mature

Emotional maturity is the foundation of healthy relationships and personal well-being. It involves self-awareness, self-regulation, empathy, and effective communication. Take responsibility for your emotions and reactions, instead of blaming others. Develop resilience in the face of adversity and learn from your experiences. Cultivate empathy towards others, seeking to understand their perspectives and feelings. Emotional maturity fosters deeper connections and enriches every aspect of your life.

Practicing Empathy in Human Relationships
Empathy is the cornerstone of meaningful relationships. It involves listening with an open heart, validating others' emotions, and offering support without judgment. Practice active listening, putting yourself in the other person's shoes, and responding with compassion and understanding. Cultivate empathy not only towards loved ones but also towards strangers and colleagues. By fostering a culture of empathy, you create a world where everyone feels seen, heard, and valued.

In conclusion, the journey towards breaking negative thought patterns and nurturing positivity is an ongoing process that requires dedication, self-reflection, and intentional action. By staying connected with loved ones, choosing happiness thoughts, mastering the art of inner speech, and practicing empathy, you can cultivate a life filled with growth, fulfilment, and meaningful relationships.

The Fundamental Right to Wealth

From the moment we are born, we are endowed with certain inalienable rights that form the cornerstone of our existence and the bedrock of our societies. Among these rights is the often-overlooked but essential right to be rich. Wealth, in its true essence, extends beyond mere monetary accumulation. It encompasses the ability to live life to its fullest potential, the freedom to pursue our passions, and the means to contribute meaningfully to the world around us.

To claim the right to be rich is to acknowledge that each individual deserves to experience the abundance that life has to offer. It is not a matter of greed but one of personal fulfillment and societal contribution. Wealth provides the resources to support our families, pursue our dreams, and foster communities. When individuals thrive financially, they can invest in education, health, and innovation, creating a ripple effect that benefits society as a whole.

The Law of Attraction and Condemnation

Our beliefs and attitudes toward wealth significantly influence our ability to attain it. This principle is deeply rooted in the law of attraction, which posits that like attracts like. Positive thoughts and attitudes draw positive experiences and opportunities, while negative thoughts repel them. This law operates on the premise that the universe responds to the energy we emit.

When we condemn money and wealth, we create a mental and emotional barrier that repels financial abundance. Condemnation stems from deeply ingrained beliefs and attitudes that view wealth as inherently evil or corrupting. These beliefs often arise from societal conditioning, cultural narratives, or personal experiences. However, the act of condemnation itself is a powerful deterrent to attracting wealth.

By condemning money, we send a signal to our subconscious mind that wealth is undesirable. This mindset shapes our actions, decisions, and ultimately, our reality. For instance, someone who believes that wealth is the root of all evil may unconsciously sabotage their financial success, avoid opportunities for growth, or engage in behaviors that ensure they remain in a state of lack.

Transforming Beliefs to Embrace Wealth

To overcome the barrier of condemnation and attract wealth, it is essential to transform our beliefs and attitudes towards money. This transformation begins with recognizing and challenging the negative narratives that have taken root in our minds. Here are some steps to help shift your mindset:

1. **Acknowledge Your Beliefs:** Take an honest inventory of your beliefs about money and wealth. Write them down and examine their origins. Are these beliefs serving you, or are they holding you back?
2. **Reframe Negative Beliefs:** Replace negative beliefs with positive affirmations. For example, change "Money is the root of all evil" to "Money is a tool for creating good in the world."
3. **Visualize Abundance:** Use visualization techniques to imagine yourself living a life of abundance. See yourself achieving your financial goals, enjoying prosperity, and contributing positively to society.
4. **Practice Gratitude:** Cultivate a habit of gratitude for the wealth you currently have, no matter how small. Gratitude shifts your focus from lack to abundance, opening the door to more positive experiences.
5. **Educate Yourself:** Gain financial literacy and understand how money works. Knowledge empowers you to make informed decisions and embrace opportunities for growth.

Embracing Wealth as a Positive Force

Wealth is a tool that can be used for tremendous good. It empowers individuals to create change, support causes they care about, and enhance their quality of life. When we view wealth through a lens of positivity and possibility, we can leverage it to build a better world.

Consider the philanthropists and entrepreneurs who have used their wealth to make significant contributions to society. Their wealth has enabled them to impact education, healthcare, poverty alleviation, and more.

By embracing the right to be rich, we acknowledge that wealth is not an end in itself but a means to achieve greater ends. It allows us to pursue our passions, support our families, and make meaningful contributions to our communities and the world at large. In this light, wealth becomes a force for good, a catalyst for positive change, and a testament to the limitless potential within each of us.

The right to be rich is an inherent aspect of our human potential. It is a recognition of our ability to achieve, thrive, and contribute meaningfully to the world. To realise this right, we must transform our beliefs and attitudes towards wealth, shedding the shackles of condemnation and embracing the possibilities of abundance. By doing so, we not only enhance our own lives but also create a ripple effect of prosperity and positivity that benefits all of humanity.

The Ageless Mind and Spirit
You Are as Young as You Think You Are
Age is often regarded as an inevitable progression, marked by the number of years since our birth. However, the concept of ageing extends far beyond the physical manifestations of wrinkles and grey hair. It is deeply rooted in our perceptions, attitudes, and beliefs about what it means to grow older. The adage "You are as young as you think you are" encapsulates the powerful role our mindset plays in determining how we experience ageing.

The mind has an extraordinary influence over our physical state. Studies in psychology and neuroscience have shown that our thoughts and beliefs can significantly impact our biological processes. When we maintain a youthful mindset, characterised by curiosity, optimism, and a willingness to embrace new experiences, we can defy the conventional expectations of ageing.

A youthful mindset is not about denying the reality of ageing but about approaching life with a spirit of vitality and resilience. It involves cultivating a sense of wonder, remaining open to learning, and staying engaged with the world around us. This perspective can lead to a more fulfilling and active life, irrespective of chronological age.

The Ageless Mind

The mind, unlike the body, does not have to succumb to the same ageing processes. While cognitive changes can occur over time, the brain's remarkable plasticity allows it to adapt and grow throughout our lives. Neuroplasticity, the brain's ability to reorganize itself by forming new neural connections, underscores the potential for continual learning and mental agility at any age.

Engaging in activities that challenge the mind can help maintain and even enhance cognitive function. Always at work, Reading, solving puzzles, learning new skills, and engaging in meaningful conversations are just a few ways to keep the mind sharp. Moreover, maintaining social connections and participating in community activities can provide mental stimulation and emotional support, further contributing to cognitive health.

Positive thinking plays a crucial role in preserving mental vitality. A positive outlook not only reduces stress but also promotes overall well-being. People who approach life with optimism and gratitude tend to experience lower levels of depression and anxiety, conditions that can exacerbate cognitive decline. By fostering a positive mindset, we can create a mental environment conducive to longevity and mental health.

The Eternal Spirit

While the body and mind are subject to change, the spirit—our core essence—remains timeless. The spirit embodies our values, passions, and purpose, transcending the physical and mental realms. It is through our spirit that we connect with a deeper sense of meaning and fulfillment in life.

Nurturing the spirit involves engaging in activities that resonate with our deepest values and aspirations. For some, this might mean pursuing creative endeavors, such as art, music, or writing. For others, it might involve spiritual practices like meditation, prayer, or spending time in nature. Acts of kindness, community service, and helping others can also nourish the spirit, providing a sense of purpose and interconnectedness. Recognizing the timeless nature of our spirit encourages us to look beyond the limitations imposed by age. It reminds us that our capacity for joy, love, and growth is not confined by our physical or mental state. By cultivating a rich inner life and aligning our actions with our core values, we can experience a sense of agelessness that transcends the years.

Practical Steps to Embrace an Ageless Life
To embrace the ageless nature of your mind and spirit, consider incorporating the following practices into your daily life:

1. **Maintain a Positive Mindset:** Practice gratitude, focus on the positive aspects of life, and challenge negative thoughts. A positive outlook can enhance your overall well-being and resilience.
2. **Engage in Lifelong Learning:** Continuously seek out new knowledge and experiences. Take up new hobbies, attend workshops, and remain curious about the world around you.
3. **Stay Physically Active:** Regular at work, physical activity supports both mental and physical health. Exercise promotes brain health, reduces stress, and improves mood.
4. **Foster Social Connections:** Build and maintain meaningful relationships. Engage with family, friends, and your community to create a supportive social network.
5. **Nurture Your Spirit:** Spend time on activities that align with your values and passions. Engage in practices that bring you joy, peace, and a sense of purpose.
6. **Practice Mindfulness and Meditation:** Cultivate awareness of the present moment through mindfulness and meditation. These practices can reduce stress and enhance your connection with your inner self.
7. **Embrace Change:** Be open to change and adaptable in your approach to life. Embracing new experiences and perspectives can keep your mind and spirit vibrant.

My friend from Pune joined a foundation at the age of 69 to assist researchers in filing patents for their innovations.

Immersed in this vibrant environment, he meets new concepts and innovators daily, enriching his understanding and staying intellectually engaged. Beyond providing administrative support, he delivers lectures on how these researchers can commercialise their patents, offering valuable insights drawn from his extensive experience. His work not only aids the scientific community but also keeps his own mind active and inspired.

The journey of ageing is as much a mental and spiritual experience as it is a physical one. By embracing the belief that "you are as young as you think you are" and recognising that your mind and spirit do not grow old, you can unlock a life of perpetual growth, joy, and fulfilment. Age becomes a state of mind, not a limiting factor. Through positive thinking, continuous learning, and nurturing your spirit, you can live an ageless life that transcends the boundaries of time.

Chapter 4: Develop Thought Engine

Our thoughts are the fuel that propels us into action, driving every decision we make and every step we take. By consciously reorganizing our thought processes, we have the opportunity to streamline our actions and simplify execution. This reorganization serves as the catalyst for unlocking greater creativity, resilience, and problem-solving abilities within ourselves. When we take control of our thoughts, we unlock the potential to navigate life's challenges with ingenuity and adaptability, ultimately leading to greater fulfillment and growth.

Six easy steps. See, Observe, Be keen, Challenge the observation, Write the problem statement, and Build the team.

Step 1. See: Identifying the Path

Once we pinpoint the problem or obstruction on our brain map, it's essential to refer back to Chapter One to grasp key factors. These factors include:

A. As of Today Business Comprehensive Evaluation
- Market Analysis: Understanding market trends and consumer behavior.
- Financial Health: Assessing the financial stability and profitability of the business.
- Product/Service Evaluation: Analyzing the strengths and weaknesses of offerings.
- Customer Analysis: Identifying target demographics and customer satisfaction levels.
- Operational Efficiency: Evaluating processes to enhance productivity and reduce costs.
- Brand Perception: Gauging how the brand is perceived by consumers and stakeholders.
- SWOT Analysis: Assessing strengths, weaknesses, opportunities, and threats.

B. Your Perception of Business
- Vision and Mission: Defining the long-term goals and purpose of the business.
- Strengths and Weaknesses: Identifying internal capabilities and areas for improvement.
- Value Proposition: Communicating the unique value offered to customers.

- Brand Identity: Establishing the personality and image of the brand.
- Growth Potential: Assessing opportunities for expansion and development.
- Challenges and Opportunities: Anticipating obstacles and potential avenues for growth.
- Emotional Connection: Fostering emotional engagement with customers and stakeholders.

C. Personal Growth

- Self-identity: Understanding one's own identity and values.
- Self-Worth: Recognizing one's inherent value and capabilities.
- Self-Image: Perceiving oneself and managing self-perception.
- Self-Reflection: Engaging in introspection and self-assessment.
- Self-Compassion: Cultivating kindness and understanding towards oneself.
- Self-confidence: Building belief in one's abilities and potential.
- Self-Development: Pursuing continuous growth and learning.

D. Self-Assessment

- Alignment with Values: Ensuring actions align with personal and organizational values.
- Impact on Others: Considering the effects of decisions on stakeholders.
- Goal Progression: Tracking progress towards personal and business objectives.
- Learning and Growth: Embracing opportunities for development and improvement.
- Intentionality: Acting with purpose and mindfulness.
- Emotional Well-being: Prioritising mental and emotional health.
- Ethical Considerations: Upholding ethical standards in decision-making.

Step 2. Observation for Seeking Solutions:

Observation is indispensable when navigating hurdles or seeking avenues for enhancement. Whether leveraging existing skill sets or recruiting new talents, observation allows for a thorough examination of various facets of the business. Drawing on insights from Chapter 2, this process aids in identifying key areas such as market dynamics, customer preferences, operational inefficiencies, and strategic opportunities.

Observation in Seeking Solutions

Observation serves as a cornerstone in the quest for solutions, offering invaluable insights and guiding decisions in navigating hurdles and pursuing avenues for enhancement. This chapter explores the pivotal role of observation in identifying and addressing challenges while uncovering opportunities for growth and improvement across various aspects of business operations.

Harnessing Existing Skills and Talents:

Observation is seeing it for the first time. it begins by taking stock of existing skills and talents within the organization. By keenly observing the capabilities of team members and assessing their strengths and weaknesses, leaders can strategically deploy resources to maximize efficiency and productivity. This process not only optimizes performance but also fosters a culture of empowerment and collaboration.

Uncovering Market Dynamics:

A keen eye for observation enables businesses to decipher the ever-evolving landscape of market dynamics. By closely monitoring industry trends, competitor strategies, and consumer behavior, organizations can proactively adapt their offerings to meet changing demands and stay ahead of the curve. Through systematic observation, businesses can identify emerging opportunities and anticipate potential threats, positioning themselves for sustainable growth and competitiveness.

Understanding Customer Preferences:

Observation plays a pivotal role in understanding the nuanced preferences and needs of customers. By observing consumer behavior, feedback, and purchasing patterns, businesses can tailor their products and services to better align with customer expectations. This customer-centric approach fosters loyalty, enhances satisfaction, and drives long-term success in a highly competitive marketplace.

Identifying Operational Inefficiencies:

Observation shines a light on operational inefficiencies that may be hindering business performance. By closely scrutinizing workflows, processes, and systems, organizations can identify bottlenecks, streamline operations, and improve overall efficiency. Through systematic observation and analysis, businesses can unlock hidden opportunities for cost savings, resource optimisation, and enhanced productivity.

Spotting Strategic Opportunities:

Observation paves the way for spotting strategic opportunities that may otherwise go unnoticed. By observing industry trends, market gaps, and emerging technologies, businesses can capitalize on untapped markets, diversify revenue streams, and drive innovation. This forward-thinking approach enables organizations to position themselves as industry leaders and seize opportunities for long-term growth and sustainability.

In conclusion, observation serves as a guiding compass in the journey of seeking solutions across various facets of business operations. By harnessing the power of observation to leverage existing skills, uncover market dynamics, understand customer preferences, identify operational inefficiencies, and spot strategic opportunities, businesses can navigate challenges effectively and unlock their full potential for success and growth.

Step 3. The Art of Keen Observation:

A keen eye for detail enables businesses to elevate product quality, optimize operations, manage finances effectively, explore untapped markets, and mend relationships with stakeholders. By closely monitoring these aspects, organizations can stay agile and responsive to evolving market trends and consumer needs.

A cornerstone of successful businesses lies in their ability to observe and interpret the intricate details that shape their operations and relationships. This chapter delves into the importance of keen observation as Step 3 in the journey towards organizational excellence. By honing a keen eye for detail, businesses can elevate product quality, optimize operations, manage finances effectively, explore untapped markets, and mend relationships with stakeholders. Through diligent observation, organizations can stay agile and responsive to evolving market trends and consumer needs, positioning themselves for sustained success and growth.

Elevating Product Quality:

Keen observation allows businesses to scrutinize every aspect of their products, from design to manufacturing, to ensure exceptional quality. By paying attention to customer feedback, product performance data, and industry benchmarks, organizations can identify areas for improvement and implement changes to enhance product quality and customer satisfaction. This commitment to excellence fosters trust and loyalty among customers, driving repeat business and positive brand perception.

Optimizing Operations:
In the pursuit of efficiency and productivity, keen observation plays a crucial role in identifying inefficiencies and streamlining processes. By closely monitoring workflows, resource allocation, and performance metrics, businesses can pinpoint bottlenecks and implement strategies to improve operational effectiveness. This continuous improvement mindset enables organizations to optimize resource utilization, reduce costs, and enhance overall efficiency, ultimately driving bottom-line results.

Managing Finances Effectively:
Financial health is fundamental to the success of any organization, and keen observation is key to maintaining sound fiscal management. By meticulously tracking expenses, revenue streams, and cash flow patterns, businesses can gain valuable insights into their financial performance and make informed decisions to mitigate risks and seize opportunities. Through vigilant monitoring and analysis, organizations can ensure financial stability and sustainability in an ever-changing economic landscape.

Exploring Untapped Markets:
Opportunities for growth abound for businesses that are attuned to market dynamics and consumer preferences. Keen observation allows organizations to identify emerging trends, niche markets, and unmet needs that present lucrative opportunities for expansion. By conducting market research, analyzing competitor strategies, and leveraging customer insights, businesses can develop tailored approaches to penetrate new markets and diversify their revenue streams, unlocking new avenues for growth and innovation.

Mending Relationships with Stakeholders:
Strong relationships with stakeholders are essential for the long-term success of any business. Keen observation enables organizations to identify issues, concerns, and opportunities for improvement in their interactions with customers, suppliers, employees, and other stakeholders. By actively listening to feedback, addressing grievances, and fostering open communication, businesses can cultivate trust, loyalty, and mutual respect, laying the foundation for collaborative partnerships and sustained success.

In conclusion, Step 3: Keen Observation, is instrumental in guiding businesses towards excellence in product quality, operational efficiency, financial management, market expansion, and stakeholder engagement. By cultivating a culture of observation and continuous improvement, organizations can adapt and thrive in an increasingly competitive and dynamic business environment, positioning themselves as leaders in their industries and driving sustainable growth and success.

Step 4. Embracing Challenge Observation:

Facing challenges head-on requires innovative thinking and a willingness to redesign processes and systems. Through challenge observation, businesses can devise novel methods, streamline workflows, implement accountability measures such as daily reporting, quantify performance metrics, and establish Key Performance Indicators (KPIs) to track progress and ensure alignment with strategic objectives.

In the realm of business, challenges are not roadblocks but opportunities for growth and innovation. This chapter delves into the concept of challenge observation as a strategic approach to addressing obstacles and driving continuous improvement. By embracing challenges head-on, businesses can harness the power of innovative thinking and process redesign to overcome hurdles and achieve their strategic objectives. Through challenge observation, organizations can devise novel methods, streamline workflows, implement accountability measures, quantify performance metrics, and establish Key Performance Indicators (KPIs) to track progress and ensure alignment with strategic objectives.

Innovative Thinking:
Challenge observation encourages businesses to adopt an innovative mindset when faced with obstacles. By challenging conventional wisdom and exploring new ideas and approaches, organisations can unlock creative solutions to complex problems. Whether it's reimagining product offerings, redesigning processes, or exploring alternative revenue streams, innovative thinking enables businesses to adapt and thrive in dynamic and competitive environments.

Redesigning Processes and Systems:
Facing challenges often necessitates a fundamental reevaluation of existing processes and systems. Through challenge observation, businesses can identify inefficiencies, bottlenecks, and areas for improvement in their operations. Organizations can optimize performance and drive tangible results by redesigning processes and systems to eliminate redundancies, streamline workflows, and enhance efficiency.

Implementing Accountability Measures:
Accountability is essential for driving progress and achieving goals. Challenge observation involves implementing accountability measures such as daily reporting and regular performance reviews to track progress and ensure accountability at all levels of the organization.
By holding individuals and teams accountable for their actions and outcomes, businesses can foster a culture of responsibility and drive performance excellence.

Quantifying Performance Metrics:
Measuring performance is critical for evaluating progress and identifying areas for improvement. Challenge observation entails quantifying performance metrics related to key business objectives, such as sales targets, customer satisfaction scores, and operational efficiency metrics. By collecting and analyzing data, businesses can gain valuable insights into their performance and make data-driven decisions to drive continuous improvement.

Establishing Key Performance Indicators (KPIs):
Key Performance Indicators (KPIs) serve as benchmarks for success and guide decision-making across the organization. Challenging the observation involves establishing KPIs that align with strategic objectives and reflect critical areas of performance. By setting clear and measurable KPIs, businesses can track progress, identify trends, and make informed decisions to drive business success.

In conclusion, challenging the observation is a strategic approach to addressing obstacles and driving continuous improvement in business operations. By embracing challenges as opportunities for growth and innovation, organizations can leverage innovative thinking, redesign processes and systems, implement accountability measures, quantify performance metrics, and establish KPIs to drive progress and achieve strategic objectives. Through challenging the observation, businesses can adapt and thrive in an ever-changing business landscape, positioning themselves for long-term success and sustainability.

Step 5. Crafting Clear Problem Statement:
Articulating clear problem statements is essential for delineating the objectives of planned actions. By succinctly defining the underlying issues, organizations can focus on addressing root causes and implementing targeted solutions. Drawing on insights gleaned from earlier chapters, businesses can align problem statements with broader strategic goals and priorities.

A crucial step in problem-solving is articulating clear and concise problem statements. This chapter delves into the importance of crafting precise problem statements to delineate the objectives of planned actions. By defining the underlying issues with clarity, organizations can direct their efforts towards addressing root causes and implementing targeted solutions. Drawing a brain map on insights gleaned from earlier chapters, businesses can align problem statements with broader strategic goals and priorities, fostering a proactive approach to problem-solving and decision-making.

Defining the Underlying Issues:
Clear problem statements serve as the foundation for effective problem-solving initiatives. They provide a succinct description of the core issues or challenges faced by the organization, enabling stakeholders to gain a comprehensive understanding of the situation at hand. By defining the underlying issues with precision, organizations can avoid ambiguity and ensure that everyone is aligned in their efforts to address the problem.

Focusing Efforts on Root Causes:
A well-crafted problem statement helps organizations to focus their efforts on addressing root causes rather than symptoms. By identifying the underlying factors contributing to the problem, businesses can develop targeted strategies to mitigate risks and drive sustainable solutions. This proactive approach ensures that resources are allocated effectively and that efforts are directed towards achieving long-term results.

Implementing Targeted Solutions:
Clear problem statements pave the way for implementing targeted solutions that address the specific needs of the organization. By clearly defining the problem at hand, businesses can identify the most appropriate course of action and develop strategies that align with their objectives and capabilities. This strategic alignment enhances the likelihood of success and enables organizations to achieve their desired outcomes efficiently.

Aligning with Strategic Goals:
Problem statements should be closely aligned with broader strategic goals
and priorities. By integrating problem-solving efforts with organizational
objectives, businesses can ensure that their actions contribute to the
overall mission and vision of the company. This alignment fosters a
cohesive approach to problem-solving and decision-making, driving
progress towards achieving long-term success.

Driving Proactive Problem-Solving:
Crafting clear problem statements encourages a proactive approach to
problem-solving within organizations. By articulating the issues at hand in
a concise and actionable manner, businesses can anticipate challenges,
identify opportunities, and take preemptive measures to address potential
risks. This proactive mindset enables organizations to stay ahead of the
curve and navigate uncertainties with confidence.

In conclusion, clear problem statements are essential for guiding effective
problem-solving initiatives within organizations. By defining the
underlying issues succinctly, businesses can focus their efforts on
addressing root causes and implementing targeted solutions that align
with broader strategic goals and priorities. Through proactive problem-
solving, organizations can anticipate challenges, seize opportunities, and
drive sustainable success in an ever-changing business landscape.

Step 6. Harnessing the Power of Team Building: Leveraging Resources
Optimal utilization of resources, including human capital, is critical for
driving growth and achieving organizational objectives. By assembling a
diverse team of skilled professionals and fostering a collaborative work
environment, businesses can tap into a wealth of expertise and creativity.
Through effective teamwork, organizations can overcome challenges,
capitalize on opportunities, and propel themselves toward sustained
success and growth hacking.

Building a cohesive and effective team is paramount for organizations
aiming to achieve their strategic objectives and drive growth. This chapter
explores the significance of leveraging resources, including human capital,
through team building efforts. By assembling a diverse team of skilled
professionals and fostering a collaborative work environment, businesses
can tap into a wealth of expertise and creativity. Through effective
teamwork, organizations can overcome challenges, capitalise on
opportunities, and propel themselves towards sustained success and
growth hacking.

Optimal Utilization of Resources:
Effective team building begins with the optimal utilization of resources, including human capital. By identifying the strengths, skills, and talents of individual team members, organizations can strategically allocate tasks and responsibilities to maximize efficiency and productivity. This ensures that each team member contributes to the collective success of the organization, leveraging their unique abilities to drive results.

Assembling a Diverse Team:
Diversity is a cornerstone of effective team building, as it brings together individuals with varied backgrounds, perspectives, and expertise. By assembling a diverse team of professionals from different disciplines, industries, and cultural backgrounds, organizations can foster innovation, creativity, and adaptability. This diversity of thought enables teams to approach challenges from multiple angles and develop innovative solutions that drive business growth.

Fostering a Collaborative Work Environment:
A collaborative work environment is essential for effective team building and resource utilization. Promotion of open communication, trust, and respect among team members, organizations can create a culture of collaboration where ideas are freely exchanged, feedback is welcomed, and teamwork is celebrated. This collaborative spirit fosters synergy and cohesion within the team, enabling individuals to work together towards common goals with shared purpose and commitment.

Overcoming Challenges and Capitalizing on Opportunities:
Effective teamwork enables organizations to overcome challenges and capitalize on opportunities with agility and resilience. This collaborative approach empowers teams to overcome obstacles, learn from failures, and continuously improve their performance.

Propelling Towards Sustained Success and Growth Hacking:
Ultimately, effective team building is instrumental in propelling organisations towards sustained success and growth hacking. Leveraging the collective wisdom and problem-solving prowess of their team members, companies can adeptly steer through uncertainties, adjust to shifts in market dynamics, and capitalize on prospects for expansion and innovation. This collaborative and agile approach enables organizations to innovate, disrupt industries, and achieve their strategic objectives in an ever-changing business landscape.

In conclusion, effective team building is essential for leveraging resources and driving growth within organizations. Creating teams with a mix of backgrounds, promoting a culture of cooperation, and championing open communication and mutual trust enables organizations to draw upon their collective human assets. This approach empowers them to tackle challenges head-on, seize emerging opportunities, and fuel a trajectory of sustainable success and innovation in the digital landscape.

Simplified thoughts serve as the potent fuel for fostering growth, providing the power necessary to propel businesses forward in their pursuit of expansion and growth. Just as a Battery Management System (BMS) optimizes performance in electric vehicles and engine air and fuel filters ensure the high efficiency and effectiveness of diesel cars, The Brain Map acts as a strategic guide, streamlining operations and maximizing productivity in Growth hacking. This structured approach enables businesses to navigate obstacles, seize opportunities, and achieve sustainable growth.

The Path to Success: Measuring Success with Happiness

Success is a multi-faceted journey that extends beyond mere achievements and accolades. True success encompasses fulfillment, growth, and a sense of purpose. In this chapter, we'll explore the steps to success, emphasizing the importance of measuring success through the lens of happiness and how happiness catalyzes growth.

Steps to Success

- **Define Your Vision:** Success begins with a clear vision of what you want to achieve. Take the time to clarify your goals, both short-term and long-term. Visualize your ideal future and set actionable steps to move closer to your vision.
- **Set SMART Goals:** Make your goals Specific, Measurable, Achievable, Relevant, and Time-bound. Break down larger goals into smaller, manageable tasks to maintain momentum and track progress effectively.
- **Take Consistent Action:** Success is the result of consistent effort and perseverance. Develop habits that align with your goals and commit to taking daily actions that move you closer to success. Embrace challenges as opportunities for growth and learning.
- **Seek Knowledge and Feedback:** Continuously educate yourself and seek feedback from mentors, peers, and experts in your field. Be open to constructive criticism and use it to refine your approach and improve your skills.

- **Adapt and Innovate:** The path to success is rarely linear. Be flexible and adaptable in the face of obstacles and setbacks. Embrace change as an opportunity to innovate and evolve your strategies.
- **Cultivate Resilience:** Success often requires resilience in the face of adversity. Develop coping mechanisms to navigate challenges and setbacks with grace and determination. Remember that failure is not the opposite of success but a stepping stone towards it.
- **Pay back to society:** Paying back to society is an essential aspect of personal and collective success. As individuals, we are interconnected with our communities and have a responsibility to contribute positively to the welfare of others. Whether through volunteering, philanthropy, or advocating for social change, paying back to society not only benefits those in need but also enriches our own lives. By sharing our time, resources, and expertise, we create a ripple effect of goodwill and empowerment that uplifts society as a whole. Furthermore, fostering a culture of giving and compassion strengthens the social fabric and promotes a more equitable and sustainable future for generations to come. In essence, paying back to society is not just a moral obligation but a transformative act that embodies the essence of true success.

Measure Your Success with Happiness
While traditional metrics of success such as wealth, status, and accomplishments are important, they do not necessarily guarantee happiness. True success is measured by the level of fulfilment and contentment you experience in your life. Consider the following aspects when measuring your success:

Quality of Relationships: Strong, meaningful relationships contribute significantly to happiness and overall well-being. Evaluate the quality of your relationships with family, friends, and colleagues, and prioritize nurturing connections that bring you joy and support.

Sense of Purpose: Success is deeply intertwined with having a sense of purpose and meaning in life. Reflect on whether your actions align with your values and passions. Cultivate activities and pursuits that bring a sense of fulfillment and contribution to the world.

Work-Life Balance: Achieving success should not come at the expense of your health and well-being. Strive to maintain a healthy balance between work, leisure, and self-care. Prioritize activities that recharge and rejuvenate you, allowing you to perform at your best.

Personal Growth and Development: Success is not just about reaching a destination but also about the journey of growth and self-improvement. Measure your success by the progress you make towards becoming the best version of yourself. Celebrate your achievements and milestones, no matter how small.

Happiness: The Hack to Growth

Happiness is not just the outcome of success; it is also the catalyst for growth and achievement. When you approach life with a positive mindset and prioritize happiness, you unlock your full potential and attract opportunities for success. Here's how happiness fuels growth:

- **Enhanced Creativity and Innovation:** Happy individuals are more creative and innovative, as they are open to new ideas and perspectives. Cultivate a joyful mindset to unleash your creative potential and find innovative solutions to challenges.

- **Increased Resilience:** Happiness acts as a buffer against stress and adversity, allowing you to bounce back stronger from setbacks. Cultivate resilience by nurturing a positive outlook and focusing on gratitude and optimism.

- **Boosted Productivity and Performance:** Happy individuals are more productive and perform better in their endeavors. When you prioritize happiness, you increase your energy, focus, and motivation, leading to higher levels of performance and achievement.

- **Stronger Relationships:** Happiness is contagious and strengthens your connections with others. Cultivate a joyful presence and spread positivity in your interactions, building a supportive network that fosters growth and success.

The Resurgence of Happiness

The Turning Point

My businessman friend had reached a low point after his business failure, burdened by debts and facing an uncertain future. The journey to pay back every penny he owed was drain and exhausting, but it was a path he had chosen to walk with determination. As he navigated through this challenging phase, he made a pivotal decision that would redefine his life: he decided to make happiness a habit.

Cultivating Joy in Small Wins

He understood that happiness didn't have to come from monumental
achievements alone.

My friend began celebrating every small victory, whether it was making a
single sale or filing a patent for a new product idea. These moments of joy
became the fuel that powered his resilience. By shifting his focus from the
pressure of large-scale success to the satisfaction of incremental progress, He
transformed his outlook on life and business.

Building a Debt-Free Empire

As his mindset shifted, so did his fortunes. With each debt repaid, he felt
lighter and more empowered. He was no longer bogged down by financial
constraints or the fear of failure. This newfound freedom allowed him to
rebuild his business with a clear, strategic vision. He was meticulous in his
approach, ensuring that every step he took was grounded in solid financial
principles to avoid falling back into debt.

Growth through Innovation

His happiness-driven approach sparked a wave of creativity and
innovation. He was passionate about developing products that were not
only marketable but also unique and useful. Filing patents became a
regular part of his business strategy, securing his innovations and
providing a competitive edge in the market. His ability to innovate became
a cornerstone of his business, propelling its growth exponentially.

The Fruits of Resilience

Today, He is a testament to the power of resilience and a positive mindset.
His business has grown multifold, standing as a beacon of success in
Nashik. He runs his company with no debt, a remarkable achievement that
speaks volumes about his strategic acumen and financial discipline. His
story is not just one of financial success but also a narrative of personal
growth and happiness.

The Habit of Happiness

His success can be attributed to his deliberate choice to cultivate
happiness. By celebrating small wins and maintaining a positive outlook,
he created an environment where joy and innovation thrived. His habit of
happiness not only sustained him through difficult times but also became
the foundation upon which he rebuilt his life and business.

My friend's journey from a failed businessman laden with debt to a thriving entrepreneur in Nashik is an inspiring tale of transformation. It underscores the importance of a brain map, a positive mindset, and the power of small, consistent steps towards a larger goal.

His story teaches us that happiness is not just a fleeting emotion but a habit that can be cultivated and nurtured to drive success and fulfillment in all aspects of life.

In conclusion, success is not solely determined by external achievements but by the level of happiness and fulfillment, you experience in your life. By following the steps to success and measuring your progress through the lens of happiness, you unlock the key to sustainable growth, resilience, and lasting fulfilment. Embrace happiness as the ultimate hack to unlocking your full potential and achieving true success.

Chapter 5: Grow Your Business with Your Power Centre

Business growth and personal growth are not separate entities; rather, they are intertwined in a symbiotic relationship. To achieve sustainable and meaningful growth in business, it's crucial to align our professional endeavors with our inherent strengths. By recognizing and leveraging our unique skills and abilities, we can maximize our potential and drive innovation within our organizations. Strategies such as investing in continuous learning, fostering a growth mindset, and seeking opportunities for personal development can propel both individual and business growth forward.

Mastering Sales Success through Clarity - Profit first maintaining top-line growth

In the dynamic world of sales, success often hinges on the ability to navigate through complex tasks with clarity and precision.
My friend explored the journey as a sales head who, despite being proficient in online sales, faced challenges when inundated with multiple instructions for a single task. Through the lens of a brain map, he uncovered the power of clarity in decision-making and its transformative impact on sales performance.
When the brain map was observed thoroughly, it became evident that his ability to accomplish tasks was strong; however, his belief in pursuing multiple options for completing a single task was introducing unnecessary complexity. This approach not only led to the overuse of resources but also resulted in inefficiencies that hampered execution. Despite his proficiency as a task master, this tendency to explore numerous avenues simultaneously created barriers to growth. Instead of streamlining processes and focusing on optimal solutions, he inadvertently wasted resources and stifled potential progress.

- **The Conundrum of Multiple Instructions:**

My friend, a skilled sales professional, found himself overwhelmed when confronted with numerous instructions for a single task. Despite his proficiency in online sales, the abundance of options left him struggling to determine the most effective course of action. Recognizing the need for clarity, he embarked on a growth journey to simplify his decision-making process.

- **Unveiling the Power of Brain Mapping:**

In his quest for clarity, our sales head turned to the innovative strategy of brain mapping. By visually plotting multiple options for completing the task, he gained invaluable insights into the intricacies of each approach. Some options emerged with clarity and smooth flow, while others appeared convoluted, indicating potential pitfalls and dependencies.

- **Harnessing Clarity for Confident Decision-Making:**

Armed with a comprehensive overview of his options, our sales head delved deeper into the analysis, evaluating each scenario's strengths, weaknesses, opportunities, and threats (SWOT). With clarity as his compass, he honed in on the option that resonated most with his instincts and expertise. By aligning his gut feeling with strategic clarity, he fortified his confidence in achieving multifold growth.

- **The Path to Exponential Growth:**

With clarity as his guiding principle, our sales head embarked on a transformative journey, leveraging the power of brain mapping to optimize his decision-making process. As a result, he achieved a remarkable 2.5 times increase in sales within seven months, all without the need for additional team members. By choosing the best-suited option with the aid of brain mapping, he unlocked his full potential and propelled his sales performance to new heights.

The experience of my friend serves as a testament to the profound impact of clarity on sales success. In a world rife with complexities and uncertainties, clarity emerges as the cornerstone of confident decision-making and exponential growth. By embracing the power of brain mapping and leveraging clarity as a guiding force, sales professionals can unlock their true potential and achieve unparalleled success in their endeavors.

Crafting Success in Construction Sales Through Customer Insight

In the competitive realm of construction, achieving sales success requires more than just confidence in one's product—it demands a deep understanding of the customer's needs and motivations. This part delves into the journey of my friend, a construction builder who, despite his confidence in his constructions, struggled to convert visitors into buyers. Through the lens of brain mapping, we explore the transformative power of customer insight in driving sales growth.

- **The Challenge of Sales Conversion:**

Our builder friend faced a daunting challenge in selling his new venture of 200 homes. Driven by a desire to sell to every visitor, he found himself inundated with inquiries but saw disappointingly low sales figures. Despite his conviction in the quality of his homes, he struggled to connect with potential buyers on a deeper level.

- **Unlocking Customer Insights through Brain Mapping:**

Recognizing the need for a paradigm shift, our builder friend turned to the innovative strategy of brain mapping to gain clarity on his customer base. By visualizing his previous customers' profiles and behaviors, he unearthed valuable insights into their needs, preferences, and purchasing motivations. Armed with this newfound understanding, he set out to redefine his approach to sales.

- **Targeting the Right Customers with Precision:**

With a comprehensive customer profile in hand, our builder friend made a strategic shift in his sales strategy. Instead of casting a wide net and hoping for the best, he focused his efforts on targeting customers who aligned closely with his ideal buyer persona. By honing in on individuals who exhibited similar characteristics to his past customers, he maximized his chances of success.

- **Driving Sales Growth through Informed Decision-Making:**

Empowered by customer insight, our builder friend embarked on a journey of targeted sales efforts. Leveraging the lessons learned from his brain map, he tailored his marketing messages and sales pitches to resonate with the specific needs and desires of his target audience. As a result, he witnessed a dramatic uptick in sales, closing deals that accumulated to the total of the past three years within a mere four months.

My friend, a construction builder serves as a testament to the transformative power of customer insight in driving sales success. By leveraging brain mapping to gain a deeper understanding of his customer base, he was able to pivot his approach and achieve remarkable results.

My builder friend was struggling with sales for his new venture of 200 homes. Eager to sell a home to everyone visiting his construction site, he operated under the assumption that "customers need homes desperately and I am the only option." This mindset blinded him to the specific needs and motivations of his potential buyers, resulting in many visitors but very few sales. Although confident in his product, he lacked insight into his walk-in customers. I advised him to create a customer profile based on those who had purchased apartments in the past years. By delving into his brain map, he gained a deeper understanding of his strengths and the areas where he needed to improve. This focused approach enabled him to identify and target the right customers, leading to a dramatic increase in sales. In just four months, he closed deals equivalent to the total sales of the past three years, demonstrating the power of a well-defined customer profile and strategic marketing.

Expanding Horizons: A Journey of Exploration in Export Business

In the dynamic world of export business, success often lies in the ability to embrace change and explore new opportunities. This part delves into the story of my friend, an experienced exporter who, armed with funds and years of industry expertise, embarked on a quest to expand his business into new territories and commodities. Through the lens of brain mapping, he uncover the transformative power of curiosity, adaptability, and strategic planning in driving export growth.

- **The Urge for Expansion:**

Our exporter friend, fuelled by a desire for new challenges and growth, found himself at a crossroads in his export journey. Despite his considerable experience and ample financial resources, he grappled with the question of which products to venture into and which countries to target. Armed with an extensive market research report, he sought clarity and direction for his ambitious expansion plans.

- **Navigating Complexity through Brain Mapping:**

In his quest for clarity, our exporter friend turned to the innovative strategy of brain mapping to untangle his thoughts and aspirations. As he visualized his business plan and aspirations, he unearthed a blend of excitement for new ventures and apprehension about entering unfamiliar territories. Despite his eagerness for novelty, he hesitated when considering the prospect of exploring new countries.

- **Embracing Confidence and Familiarity:**

Drawing insights from his brain map, our exporter friend realized the importance of leveraging his existing connections and expertise. Recognizing his confidence in his established networks in countries where he had previously exported, he devised a strategic plan to revisit these territories. By immersing himself in these markets for an extended period, he aimed to uncover opportunities for new products and forge fresh connections while nurturing existing ones.

- **Cultivating Success through Strategic Exploration:**

Armed with a renewed sense of purpose and a strategic plan, our exporter friend embarked on an immersive journey into his strongholds. Over the course of three months, he delved deep into the market dynamics, identified emerging trends, and fostered relationships with potential partners and customers. Through a blend of perseverance, adaptability, and strategic networking, he successfully diversified his product portfolio and expanded his business multifold in just two years.

Our exporter friend in Hong Kong serves as a testament to brain mapping's transformative power of strategic exploration in the export business. By embracing familiarity while venturing into the unknown, he unlocked new avenues of growth and success.

Our exporter friend was eager to venture into new commodities and countries. With additional funds sanctioned by banks and 15 years of experience in the export business, his main question was, "What products for which countries?" He even had an in-depth report from a global market research company, likely paying a significant amount for it. I suggested he create a brain map of his new business plan. Through this process, it became clear that he was tired of the routine and craved new challenges and a diversified portfolio, even if it meant risking money for new learning experiences. He wanted to enroll in new ventures and achieve great success. However, his brain map also revealed a lack of confidence in exporting to new countries. Based on this insight, I advised him to leverage his confidence in his existing connections in countries he had previously exported to. By spending three months in these countries, he could explore the potential of new products from the market research report and forge new first-degree and second-degree connections. This strategy led to his business growing multifold over two years, as he successfully added new products to his portfolio and strengthened his network in familiar territories. In an ever-evolving landscape where adaptability and curiosity are paramount, exporters can draw inspiration from his journey to navigate complexities, seize opportunities, and chart a course towards sustainable expansion and prosperity.

Unleashing Potential: Finding Your Niche as a Columnist

In the realm of freelance writing and columnist, the quest for the next topic can often be a daunting one. This part follows the journey of a freelance writer and columnist as she navigates the intricate landscape of her craft. Through the lens of a brain map and her experience, we explore the transformative power of self-discovery and niche exploration in unlocking her true potential as a writer.

- **The Quest for Inspiration:**

A talented freelance writer and columnist, met me at a conference at Mumbai, seeking fresh inspiration for her next endeavor. Despite her prowess with words, she was grappled with uncertainty, unsure of which direction to take her writing next. In her quest for clarity, she turned to her trusted confidant for guidance.

- **Navigating the Brain Map:**

Examining her brain map, we uncovered a wealth of insights into her strengths, interests, and aspirations. While she had previously delved into topics related to spiritual guidance, her brain map revealed a latent passion for exploring the intricacies of human personalities and their relationship with spirituality.

- **Discovering a Unique Perspective:**

Armed with newfound clarity, my columnist friend realized the potential for carving out a niche in writing about the intersection of personality and spirituality.

Rather than focusing solely on spiritual guides, she recognized the opportunity to delve deeper into the lives of individuals around her and explore how they incorporate spirituality into their daily lives to achieve success, growth, and fulfillment.

- **Crafting Compelling Narratives:**

With her niche identified, our columnist friend set out to weave captivating narratives that shed light on the diverse ways in which spirituality influences human behavior and decision-making. Drawing inspiration from the personalities she encountered in her daily life, she crafted insightful stories that resonated with her audience and left a lasting impact.

- **Empowering Personal and Professional Growth:**

Through her newfound focus on writing about personalities and spirituality, our columnist friend experienced a profound sense of fulfilment and purpose in her craft.

By aligning her writing with her inherent passions and strengths, she not only enriched her own life but also empowered her readers to reflect on their own spiritual journeys and embrace personal growth.

She is a freelance writer and columnist for local newspapers, and she asked me, "What next?" By examining her brain map, I helped her realize that she could excel at writing about the personalities she encounters daily, rather than focusing solely on spiritual guides. I suggested that she could make a greater impact by exploring how these individuals incorporate spirituality into their lives and achieve success. This approach would not only highlight her observational skills and storytelling ability but also offer readers relatable and inspiring content about the practical applications of spirituality in everyday life.

The journey of our columnist friend serves as a testament to the transformative power of self-discovery and niche exploration in the world of freelance writing and columnists. Exploring her passions and utilizing the knowledge gained from her brain map enabled her to tap into her innate writing talents and distinguish herself in a saturated market. Aspiring columnists looking to achieve artistic satisfaction and professional accomplishment can look to her experience for motivation, using it to fuel their dedication, define their distinctive spaces, and create a significant influence with their prose.

Navigating the Path to Public Listing: Overcoming Mental Blocks

The journey to taking a company public is often perceived as a milestone of success, yet it comes with its own set of challenges and mental barriers. This chapter delves into the story of a friend business owner's quest to list his company on the stock exchange and raise funds through an Initial Public Offering (IPO). Through the lens of a brain map and his experience, we explore the transformative power of identifying and overcoming mental blocks to achieve financial growth and professional success.

- **The Ambitious Goal of Going Public:**

Our protagonist, a successful business owner with a thriving company, harbored aspirations of taking his enterprise public and accessing capital through the stock market. With a solid track record of profitability and a clear vision for growth, he set his sights on an ambitious 18-month timeline to achieve this milestone. However, as he embarked on this journey, he encountered unexpected hurdles that threatened to derail his plans.

- **Unraveling Mental Blocks:**

In a pivotal meeting in Delhi, our protagonist candidly shared his struggles with closing deals with High Net Worth Individuals (HNIs) for investment in his company's IPO. Examining his brain map, it be came evident that he harbored deep-seated hesitations and fears surrounding borrowing money and relinquishing control of his business to investors. These mental blocks stemmed from a history of self-reliance and a reluctance to engage in the complexities of corporate politics.

- **Harnessing the Power of Brain Mapping:**

Armed with insights from his brain map, our protagonist embarked on a journey of self-discovery and growth. By acknowledging and addressing his mental barriers head-on, he gained a newfound clarity and determination to navigate the intricacies of the IPO process. Recognizing the need for professional guidance, he sought the expertise of merchant bankers and company secretaries to demystify the complexities of managing a listed company and cultivating investor relationships.

- **Embracing a Transformational Mindset:**

Through the process of introspection and professional support, our protagonist underwent a profound transformation in his mindset and approach to wealth creation. Shifting from the mindset of a sole proprietor to that of a major shareholder in his own company, he embraced a newfound sense of wealth consciousness and strategic thinking. By reframing his relationship with investors as purely professional and profit-driven, he overcame his fears of losing control and harnessed the power of collaboration for mutual benefit.

Achieving Transformation and Success:
Armed with a newfound sense of confidence and clarity, my friend successfully navigated the complexities of the IPO process and achieved his goal of listing his company on the stock exchange.

By leveraging the insights gained from his brain map and embracing a transformational mindset, he not only secured the necessary funding through IPO for growth but also positioned himself as a leader in his industry. Through overcoming mental blocks and embracing change, he unlocked his true potential for financial prosperity and professional success.

My friend, the promoter of a stock exchange-listed company, wanted to list his company and raise money through an IPO, aiming to go public within 18 months. His company had a strong turnover and good profits, meeting all the requirements for public listing. However, during a meeting in Delhi, he expressed difficulty in closing deals with HNI investors. From his brain map, I observed he had a hesitation to borrow money, as he had built his empire by reinvesting his profits and maintaining low payouts. Additionally, he feared that investors might take over his business and felt insecure about handling corporate politics. Using the brain map, he identified these mental blockages that hindered his ability to convert profits into wealth. He realized that investor relationships are purely professional, focused on profits and share price. I advised him to seek help from professionals like merchant bankers and company secretaries to manage compliance and build positive relationships with investors. Embracing wealth consciousness, he transitioned from being an "owner" to a "major shareholder" in his company. This transformation, facilitated by the brain map, enabled him to achieve his goal of going public.

The journey of my friend serves as a powerful testament to the transformative power of identifying and overcoming mental blocks on the path to success. By harnessing the insights of brain mapping and embracing a mindset of growth and collaboration, he navigated the complexities of the IPO process with confidence and achieved his ambitious goals. In the realm of business and finance, aspiring entrepreneurs can draw inspiration from their journey to confront their mental barriers and chart a course toward lasting success and fulfillment.

In the journey of business growth hacking, harnessing personal growth becomes a pivotal strategy for success.

The intertwining relationship between personal and business growth is undeniable, as demonstrated throughout this exploration. Aligning professional endeavors with inherent strengths emerges as a cornerstone for sustainable and meaningful growth.

With the recognition and leverage of unique skills and abilities, individuals and organizations can unlock their full potential. Strategies such as investing in continuous learning, fostering a growth mindset, and seeking opportunities for personal development serve as catalysts for growth hacking. When individuals are empowered to grow personally, they bring their best selves to the workplace, resulting in increased productivity, creativity, and overall success.

In essence, prioritizing personal growth alongside business growth creates a holistic approach that fosters long-term prosperity and fulfillment. As individuals and organizations continue on their journey of growth, embracing the power within their own center becomes the driving force for unlocking endless possibilities and achieving extraordinary outcomes.

Simple Thoughts: Cultivating Growth and Clarity

In the pursuit of growth and success, simplicity of thought often proves to be a formidable ally. By harnessing the power of straightforward, disciplined thinking, we can navigate complexities, cultivate wealth consciousness, and foster exponential growth without overburdening ourselves. Let's explore how simplicity of thought drives growth, promotes balance, and enhances clarity in various aspects of life.

Simple Thoughts Drive Growth

Contrary to popular belief, growth isn't solely fueled by sheer willpower or complex strategies. It often begins with simple, focused thoughts aligned with our goals and values. By breaking down daunting tasks into manageable steps and maintaining clarity of purpose, we pave the way for sustainable growth and progress.

Embracing Simplicity for Exponential Growth

The key to exponential growth lies in simplicity. By streamlining our efforts and focusing on high-impact activities, we can maximize our productivity and achieve remarkable results. Instead of spreading ourselves thin, we concentrate our energy on what truly matters, allowing growth to flourish organically.

Discipline in Thought

Discipline in thought involves consciously directing our mental focus towards productive and positive endeavors. By cultivating mental discipline, we can resist distractions, overcome self-doubt, and stay committed to our aspirations. Through consistent practice, disciplined thoughts become the foundation upon which we build success and fulfillment.

Wealth Consciousness

Wealth consciousness refers to an awareness and mindset that attracts and creates financial abundance and prosperity. It involves adopting a positive and abundant attitude towards wealth, believing in one's ability to achieve financial success, and making conscious choices that support financial well-being. This concept often includes:

Positive Mindset: Believing that wealth is achievable and maintaining a positive attitude towards money.

Financial Education: Gaining knowledge about financial management, investments, and wealth-building strategies.

Gratitude and Generosity: Practicing gratitude for what one has and being generous, can create a cycle of abundance.

Intentional Action: Setting clear financial goals and taking deliberate steps towards achieving them.

Removing Limiting Beliefs: Identifying and overcoming negative beliefs about money that may hinder financial success.

Wealth consciousness is often associated with personal development and self-improvement, emphasizing that a healthy relationship with money can lead to greater financial stability and growth.

Balancing Growth with Life

Achieving growth doesn't have to come at the expense of a balanced life. By simplifying our approach and focusing on what truly matters, we can experience exponential growth without sacrificing our well-being or relationships. It's about finding harmony between work and life, allowing growth to unfold naturally while prioritizing our overall happiness and fulfilment.

Protecting Your Power Center

Our thoughts are our most potent tool for growth, but they can also be vulnerable to external influences. By safeguarding our mental space and surrounding ourselves with positivity, we protect our power center and maintain clarity of thought. This allows us to navigate challenges with resilience and emerge stronger and wiser.

Harnessing the Power of Sleep

Sleep is not only essential for physical rejuvenation but also for mental clarity and problem-solving. By allowing our brains to rest and recharge, we gain insights and clarity that elude us during waking hours. By prioritizing quality sleep and embracing the wisdom of our dreams, we awaken with renewed vigor and growth-oriented thoughts.

Simple is scalable

"Simple is scalable" suggests that simplicity in growth hacking, design, processes, or systems enables easier scaling and expansion. When a solution is simple, it's typically easier to understand, implement, and replicate, which reduces the complexity and cost associated with scaling up operations or adapting to larger volumes. Simplicity often leads to more efficient troubleshooting, maintenance, and training, making it a strategic choice for growth. This principle is widely applied in technology, business, and project management to achieve sustainable and manageable growth.

In essence, simplicity of thought is the catalyst for growth, clarity, and balance in life. By embracing simplicity, disciplining our thoughts, and nurturing wealth consciousness, we unlock the true source of wealth and abundance within. As we protect our power center, harness the power of sleep, and embrace the growth of others, we pave the way for exponential growth and fulfilment in every aspect of our lives.

Chapter 6: Spirituality is Key Asset

Beyond material pursuits lies the realm of spirituality, a source of profound wisdom and guidance. This chapter explores the integration of spiritual principles into our personal and professional lives, enriching our journey toward growth.

The Intersection of Intelligence, Wisdom, and Spiritual Growth: Nurturing Wealth Consciousness and Collective Well-being

In the pursuit of success and growth, it's crucial to recognize the distinction between intelligence and wisdom. It is also to understand the profound impact of spirituality on our journey towards wealth consciousness and collective well-being. Let's explore how developing spiritual insight can foster both individual and communal prosperity:

The Essence of Spiritual Growth

In the pursuit of success and fulfillment, many of us equate intelligence with achievement—a measure of our ability to navigate the complexities of the world and achieve our goals. However, true growth transcends mere intellect; it is rooted in wisdom—a deep understanding of ourselves, our place in the universe, and the interconnectedness of all things. To embark on a journey of spiritual growth is to delve into the depths of our being, to cultivate awareness, compassion, and authenticity in every aspect of our lives.

Intelligence vs. Wisdom

Intelligence is the ability to acquire knowledge and solve problems—a valuable asset in the pursuit of success and achievement. However, wisdom goes beyond intellect; it is the product of experience, reflection, and insight—a guiding light that illuminates the path to true understanding and fulfillment. While intelligence may lead to success in the material world, wisdom fosters growth and transformation on a deeper, more meaningful level.

The Spiritual Journey

Spiritual growth is a journey of self-discovery and self-transcendence—a quest for meaning, purpose, and connection in a world filled with uncertainty and ambiguity. It is a journey that requires courage, humility, and a willingness to confront the depths of our being—the shadows as well as the light. Through practices such as meditation, mindfulness, and self-inquiry, we cultivate awareness and presence, deepening our understanding of ourselves and the world around us.

The Essence of Being Spiritual

Being spiritual is not about adhering to a set of beliefs or teachings or faith; it is about embodying certain qualities and values that reflect our true nature as spiritual beings. Compassion, empathy, kindness, and gratitude are among the hallmarks of spiritual growth—qualities that foster connection, understanding, and harmony in our relationships and interactions with others. Being spiritual is about living with intention and integrity, aligning our thoughts, words, and actions with our deepest values and aspirations.

The Path to Spiritual Growth

The path to spiritual growth is as unique and individual as we are. It is a journey of exploration and discovery—a quest for meaning and purpose that unfolds with each step we take. By cultivating awareness, compassion, and authenticity in every aspect of our lives, we align ourselves with the flow of life, allowing us to experience greater peace, joy, and fulfilment. Along the way, we may encounter challenges and setbacks, but each obstacle becomes an opportunity for growth and transformation—a stepping stone on the path to spiritual awakening.

Intelligence may lead to success, but wisdom fosters growth—a deeper, more profound understanding of ourselves and the world around us. Being spiritual is about embracing the journey of self-discovery and self-transcendence, cultivating awareness, compassion, and authenticity in every aspect of our lives. By aligning ourselves with the flow of life and living with intention and integrity, we embark on a journey of spiritual growth that leads to greater peace, joy, and fulfilment.

Cultivating Wealth Consciousness

In the pursuit of success and fulfilment, the concept of wealth consciousness transcends mere material riches—it encompasses a holistic approach to abundance that encompasses both material prosperity and spiritual well-being. By embracing the notion that work is worship, we can cultivate a mindset of abundance and gratitude that fosters not only financial success but also holistic well-being in every aspect of our lives.

Understanding Wealth Consciousness

Wealth consciousness is a state of mind characterized by abundance, gratitude, and a deep sense of connection to the flow of life. It is the recognition that true wealth extends beyond material possessions to encompass health, relationships, personal growth, and spiritual fulfilment. By cultivating wealth consciousness, we shift our focus from scarcity and lack to abundance and gratitude, opening ourselves up to the infinite possibilities that exist within and around us.

Work as Worship: Finding Meaning and Purpose

The notion that work is worship speaks to the inherent dignity and value of every task, no matter how mundane or challenging. When we approach our work with reverence and dedication, we infuse it with meaning and purpose, transforming even the most routine tasks into opportunities for growth and self-expression. By aligning our work with our values and aspirations, we cultivate a sense of fulfillment and satisfaction that transcends mere financial gain.

Principles for Cultivating Wealth Consciousness

1. **Gratitude:** Cultivate an attitude of gratitude for the abundance that surrounds you, both material and spiritual. Practice gratitude daily by acknowledging the blessings in your life and expressing appreciation for the people, experiences, and opportunities that enrich your journey.
2. **Abundance Mindset:** Shift your mindset from scarcity to abundance by focusing on possibilities rather than limitations. Embrace the belief that there is more than enough to go around and that success is not a zero-sum game.
3. **Purposeful Work:** Find meaning and purpose in your work by aligning it with your values, passions, and aspirations. Approach each task with dedication and enthusiasm, recognizing the opportunity for growth and self-expression that it represents.
4. **Holistic Well-Being**: Prioritize your well-being by attending to all aspects of your life—physical, mental, emotional, and spiritual. Cultivate practices such as meditation, exercise, self-care, and personal development to nurture your overall health and vitality.
5. **Contribution and Service**: Give back to others and contribute to the greater good by sharing your time, talents, and resources with those in need. Recognize the interconnectedness of all beings and the importance of collective well-being in creating a thriving, sustainable world.

Cultivating wealth consciousness and well-being is not just about accumulating material riches; it is about embracing a holistic approach to abundance that encompasses all aspects of our lives. By recognizing the inherent value and dignity of our work and approaching it with reverence and dedication, we infuse our lives with meaning and purpose. Through practices such as gratitude, abundance mindset, purposeful work, holistic well-being, and contribution to others, we create a life of abundance, fulfilment, and joy that transcends material wealth alone.

Wealth as a Tool for Social Impact

In the tapestry of human existence, wealth occupies a unique position—it is both a means to personal fulfillment and a powerful tool for driving positive change in the world. When wielded with wisdom and compassion, wealth can be a catalyst for social transformation, enabling individuals and organizations to execute their social causes with greater impact and effectiveness. By recognizing the inherent potential of wealth as a force for good, we can harness its power to create a more just, equitable, and sustainable world for all.

The Role of Wealth in Social Impact

Wealth, when viewed through the lens of service and stewardship, becomes a potent force for social impact. It provides the resources and infrastructure needed to address pressing social and environmental challenges, from poverty and inequality to climate change and access to education. Whether through philanthropy, impact investing, or corporate social responsibility, wealth empowers individuals and organizations to make meaningful contributions to the greater good, amplifying their impact and catalyzing positive change on a global scale.

The Intersection of Wealth and Purpose

Wealth is not an end in itself; rather, it is a means to an end—a tool for realizing our deepest aspirations and values. When aligned with a sense of purpose and service, wealth becomes a vehicle for expressing our values and making a meaningful difference in the world. Whether it's funding social enterprises, supporting grassroots initiatives, or advocating for policy change, wealth enables us to leverage our resources and influence for the greater good, advancing causes that are close to our hearts and aligning with our vision for a better world.

The Ethical Responsibility of Wealth

With great wealth comes great responsibility, an ethical imperative to use our resources and influence for the betterment of society and the planet. Wealthy individuals and corporations have a unique opportunity, and obligation to address systemic injustices, promote environmental sustainability, and champion the rights and dignity of all people. By adopting ethical business practices, investing in sustainable solutions, and advocating for social justice, wealth holders can play a pivotal role in creating a more equitable and compassionate world for future generations.

The Power of Collective Action

While individual wealth can drive significant social impact, the true power of wealth lies in its ability to mobilize collective action and catalyze systemic change.

By leveraging their resources and networks, wealthy individuals and organisations can inspire others to join their cause, amplifying their impact and creating a ripple effect of positive change across communities and continents. Through collaboration, cooperation, and solidarity, we can harness the full potential of wealth as a force for good, creating a more just, equitable, and sustainable world for all.

Wealth is not inherently good or evil; it is simply a tool—a means to an end. When wielded with wisdom, compassion, and a sense of purpose, wealth becomes a powerful force for social impact, enabling individuals and organisations to address pressing social and environmental challenges with greater efficacy and efficiency. By recognising the inherent potential of wealth as a catalyst for positive change, we can harness its power to create a more just, equitable, and sustainable world for all.

Harnessing the Power of Desire for Growth

Desire is a potent force—a driving energy that propels us forward on the journey of growth and self-discovery. When channeled with intention and clarity, our desires become prayers for growth—invocations to the universe that guide us towards our highest aspirations and deepest fulfilment. By harnessing the power of desire as a catalyst for growth, we unlock the full potential of our being and cultivate a life of purpose, passion, and abundance.

Understanding the Nature of Desire
Desire is the fuel that ignites the flames of aspiration and ambition within us. It is the spark of inspiration that ignites our imagination and propels us towards our goals and dreams. Whether it's the desire for success, love, fulfilment, or meaning, our deepest longings serve as beacons of guidance, guiding us towards experiences and opportunities that align with our highest good.

Desire as Prayer
In the spiritual sense, desire is more than just a fleeting impulse or craving; it is a prayer—a heartfelt plea to the universe for guidance, support, and fulfilment. When we articulate our desires with clarity and sincerity, we send a powerful signal to the cosmos, aligning ourselves with the forces of creation and manifestation. Our desires become prayers for growth—invitations for the universe to conspire in our favour and guide us towards our highest potential.

Cultivating Intentional Desire

To harness the power of desire for growth, we must cultivate intentionality and mindfulness in our desires. Rather than chasing after fleeting pleasures or external validation, we focus our attention on what truly matters to us—our values, passions, and aspirations. We clarify our intentions and align our desires with our highest values and purpose, ensuring that our prayers for growth are rooted in authenticity and integrity.

Taking Inspired Action

Desire alone is not enough to manifest our dreams; we must also take inspired action towards their realization. While aligning our thoughts, words, and actions with our desires, we create momentum toward our goals. We seize opportunities, overcome obstacles, and navigate challenges with grace and determination, knowing that every step forward brings us closer to our dreams.

Embracing Detachment

While desire is a powerful force for growth, it is also important to cultivate a sense of detachment from the outcomes of our desires. By releasing our attachment to specific outcomes and surrendering to the flow of life, we open ourselves up to unexpected opportunities and blessings that may not have been part of our original plan. We trust in the wisdom of the universe and have faith that our prayers for growth will be answered in divine timing and accordance with our highest good.

Desire is a prayer for growth—a sacred invocation that guides us toward our highest aspirations and deepest fulfillment. By harnessing the power of desire with intentionality, mindfulness, and inspired action, we unlock the full potential of our being and cultivate a life of purpose, passion, and abundance. With clarity of intention and surrender to the flow of life, we trust in the wisdom of the universe to answer our prayers for growth and lead us toward our highest potential.

Unveiling the Inner Treasure of Wealth

In the pursuit of wealth and abundance, we often look to external sources —the accumulation of material possessions, financial assets, and social status—as markers of success and fulfillment. However, true wealth resides not in the external trappings of prosperity, but within the depths of our being. By unlocking the inner treasure of wealth—the abundance of wisdom, love, and purpose that lies within us—we tap into a reservoir of richness that transcends material possessions and enriches every aspect of our lives.

The Illusion of External Wealth

In a world that equates wealth with material possessions and financial assets, it's easy to fall into the trap of chasing after external markers of success and fulfilment. We measure our worth by the size of our bank accounts, the value of our possessions, and the prestige of our social status, believing that these external trappings hold the key to happiness and fulfilment. However, the pursuit of external wealth often leads to a sense of emptiness and disillusionment, as we discover that material possessions alone cannot satisfy the deepest longings of our soul.

Discovering the Inner Treasure

True wealth resides within us, waiting to be discovered and embraced. It is the wealth of wisdom that comes from a lifetime of experience and reflection. It is the wealth of love that flows freely from the depths of our heart, enriching our relationships and nourishing our spirit. It is the wealth of purpose that gives meaning and direction to our lives, guiding us towards our highest aspirations and deepest fulfilment. When we tap into the inner treasure of wealth, we access a source of abundance that transcends the limitations of the material world and enriches every aspect of our existence.

Cultivating Inner Wealth

Cultivating inner wealth requires a shift in perspective—a willingness to look beyond the external trappings of prosperity and connect with the richness that lies within. We cultivate inner wealth through practices such as meditation, self-reflection, and mindfulness, which allow us to quiet the noise of the external world and tune into the wisdom of our own inner guidance. We cultivate inner wealth through acts of kindness, compassion, and service, which remind us of the interconnectedness of all beings and the joy that comes from giving and receiving with an open heart. We cultivate inner wealth through a commitment to living in alignment with our values and aspirations, honouring the unique gifts and talents that we each bring to the world.

Embracing the Abundance Within

As we embrace the abundance within, we discover that true wealth is not measured by the size of our bank accounts or the value of our possessions, but by the richness of our relationships, the depth of our wisdom, and the authenticity of our purpose. We realise that the treasure of wealth is not something to be acquired or possessed, but something to be cultivated and shared—a source of abundance that flows freely from the depths of our own being and enriches the world around us. With gratitude and humility, we embrace the inner treasure of wealth and allow it to guide us towards a life

The Spiritual Essence of Growth Hacking

In the dynamic landscape of business and entrepreneurship, growth
hacking has emerged as a powerful strategy for accelerating growth and
driving innovation. At its core, growth hacking is about finding creative
and unconventional ways to achieve rapid growth and scale—a process
that often involves experimentation, iteration, and data-driven decision-
making. However, beneath the surface of growth hacking lies a deeper
truth—a spiritual essence that transcends the realm of business and taps
into the timeless wisdom of the soul.

The Intersection of Spirituality and Growth

Spirituality and growth hacking may seem like unlikely ally, but upon
closer examination, we discover that they share a common foundation—a
commitment to exploration, discovery, and transformation. At its essence,
spirituality is about awakening to the deeper truths of existence and
connecting with the infinite wellspring of wisdom and creativity that lies
within us. Similarly, growth hacking is about pushing the boundaries of
what is possible, breaking free from conventional thinking, and tapping
into the unlimited potential of human ingenuity and innovation.

Extracting Spiritual Understanding

To extract spiritual understanding from the practice of growth hacking is
to recognise that true growth extends beyond mere metrics and KPIs—it is
a journey of self-discovery and self-transcendence. By approaching growth
hacking with a spirit of curiosity, openness, and humility, we create space
for inspiration and insight to flow freely, guiding us towards innovative
solutions and transformative breakthroughs. We draw upon the wisdom of
intuition, synchronicity, and serendipity, trusting in the innate
intelligence of the universe to guide us towards our highest potential.

The alignment

Alignment is key to harnessing the spiritual essence of growth hacking.
When our actions are aligned with our values, purpose, and vision, we tap
into a deeper reservoir of motivation, creativity, and resilience that
propels us towards success. By cultivating mindfulness, presence, and
intentionality in our approach to growth hacking, we create space for the
universe to work through us, aligning our efforts with the flow of life and
opening ourselves up to infinite possibilities for growth and expansion.

Embracing the Journey

The journey of growth hacking is not just about achieving rapid growth and scale—it is about embracing the process of evolution and transformation. As we extract spiritual understanding from our experiences, we come to realise that growth hacking is not just a business strategy; it is a way of being—a mindset and philosophy that permeates every aspect of our lives. By integrating spiritual principles such as presence, authenticity, and service into our approach to growth hacking, we create a more meaningful and fulfilling experience that enriches not only our businesses but also our souls.

In the fast-paced world of business and entrepreneurship, growth hacking offers a powerful framework for achieving rapid growth and scale. Yet, beneath the surface of growth hacking lies a deeper truth—a spiritual essence that transcends the realm of business and taps into the timeless wisdom of the soul. By approaching growth hacking with a spirit of curiosity, openness, and alignment, we unlock the infinite potential of human creativity and innovation, creating not only business success but also personal fulfilment and spiritual growth.

The Spiritual Neutrality of Data Mining and Analysis

In the realm of data mining and analysis, objectivity is paramount—a commitment to uncovering insights and patterns without bias or preconceived notions. Yet, achieving true objectivity requires more than just technical skill—it demands a mindset of spiritual neutrality, a state of being in which we transcend personal biases and attachments to uncover deeper truths and insights. By cultivating spiritual neutrality in our approach to data mining and analysis, we unlock the full potential of our analytical prowess and harness the transformative power of data to drive innovation and growth.

The Illusion of Objectivity

In the pursuit of data-driven insights, it's easy to fall into the trap of believing that objectivity can be achieved through technical expertise alone. However, true objectivity goes beyond the surface-level analysis of data—it requires a willingness to question assumptions, challenge beliefs, and confront biases that may cloud our judgment. Spiritual neutrality is the key to transcending these limitations, allowing us to approach data mining and analysis with an open mind and a heart free from attachment.

Cultivating Spiritual Neutrality

Spiritual neutrality is not about detachment or indifference—it is about embracing the full spectrum of human experience with equanimity and compassion. It is the ability to observe and analyse data without being swayed by personal preferences, biases, or agendas. By cultivating mindfulness, presence, and self-awareness, we create space for spiritual neutrality to emerge, allowing us to engage with data in a way that transcends the limitations of the ego and taps into the deeper wisdom of the soul.

The Power of Non-Attachment

Non-attachment is a central tenet of spiritual neutrality—a willingness to let go of attachments to outcomes, beliefs, and identities that may cloud our judgment and impede our ability to see things as they truly are. In the context of data mining and analysis, non-attachment allows us to approach data with curiosity and openness, free from the constraints of personal bias or agenda. We become like scientists, exploring the mysteries of the universe with a spirit of inquiry and wonder, unencumbered by the need for validation or recognition.

Unlocking Deeper Insights

When we approach data mining and analysis with spiritual neutrality, we unlock the full potential of our analytical prowess and tap into deeper insights and truths that transcend the limitations of the intellect. We see patterns and connections that may have eluded us before, uncovering hidden gems of wisdom and inspiration that guide us towards innovative solutions and transformative breakthroughs. By embracing spiritual neutrality, we harness the transformative power of data to drive innovation, growth, and positive change in the world.

In the world of data mining and analysis, objectivity is paramount. Yet, achieving true objectivity requires more than just technical skill—it demands a mindset of spiritual neutrality, a state of being in which we transcend personal biases and attachments to uncover deeper truths and insights. By cultivating spiritual neutrality in our approach to data mining and analysis, we unlock the full potential of our analytical prowess and harness the transformative power of data to drive innovation, growth, and positive change in the world.

The Synergy of Human Intelligence and Artificial Intelligence in Driving Exponential Growth

In the ever-evolving landscape of innovation and progress, the synergy between human intelligence (HI) and artificial intelligence (AI) has emerged as a powerful catalyst for exponential growth and advancement. While human intellect possesses unparalleled creativity, intuition, and adaptability, artificial intelligence offers unparalleled processing power, data analysis capabilities, and automation. By harnessing the complementary strengths of HI and AI, we unlock the full potential of human ingenuity and technological innovation to drive exponential growth and transformation in every sphere of human endeavour.

The Limitless Potential of Human Intelligence

Human intelligence is a marvel of evolution—a complex tapestry of cognitive abilities, emotions, and experiences that enable us to navigate the complexities of the world with grace and adaptability. Unlike artificial intelligence, which operates within predefined parameters and algorithms, human intellect possesses the capacity for creativity, intuition, and empathy—qualities that defy quantification and measurement. It is this innate capacity for innovation and insight that drives exponential growth and advancement in fields ranging from science and technology to art and literature.

The Power of Machine learning and Artificial Intelligence

Artificial intelligence, on the other hand, offers unparalleled processing power and data analysis capabilities that far exceed those of the human brain. Through machine learning, deep learning, and neural networks, AI systems can process vast amounts of data, identify patterns and trends, and make predictions with astonishing accuracy and efficiency. In fields such as finance, healthcare, and transportation, AI is revolutionising the way we work, live, and interact with the world, driving exponential growth and innovation at an unprecedented pace.

Harnessing the Synergy of Human Intelligence and Artificial Intelligence While human intelligence and artificial intelligence possess distinct strengths and capabilities, it is their synergy that holds the greatest promise for driving exponential growth and advancement. By leveraging AI to augment human intellect, we enhance our ability to process information, make decisions, and solve complex problems with greater speed and precision. From data analysis and predictive modelling to automation and optimisation, AI empowers us to unlock new frontiers of innovation and possibility, catalysing exponential growth and transformation in every aspect of our lives.

The Role of Human Intelligence in Guiding Artificial Intelligence

Despite its remarkable capabilities, artificial intelligence is not without limitations. AI systems are only as effective as the data they are trained on and the algorithms they are programmed with. Human intelligence plays a crucial role in guiding the development and deployment of AI, ensuring that these systems are ethical, responsible, and aligned with human values and aspirations. By harnessing the wisdom, empathy, and moral compass of human intellect, we can steer the trajectory of AI towards a future that serves the greater good and benefits all of humanity.

In the dynamic interplay between human intelligence and artificial intelligence, lies the potential for exponential growth and transformation on a global scale. While human intellect possesses unparalleled creativity, intuition, and adaptability, artificial intelligence offers unmatched processing power, data analysis capabilities, and automation. By harnessing the complementary strengths of HI and AI, we unlock the full potential of human ingenuity and technological innovation to drive exponential growth and advancement in every sphere of human endeavour, shaping a future that is brighter, more prosperous, and more equitable for all.

Completing the Circle of Wealth: Giving Back to Society and Team

In the pursuit of wealth and success, it's easy to get caught up in the idea of accumulation—to focus solely on acquiring more, without considering the impact of our actions on others and the world around us. However, true prosperity lies not in hoarding wealth, but in sharing it with others and giving back to the communities and teams that support us on our journey. By completing the circle of wealth—earning from society and giving back to society—we create a sustainable ecosystem of growth and prosperity that benefits everyone involved.

The Cycle of Wealth Creation

Wealth is not created in isolation—it is the product of collaboration, innovation, and exchange within society. Whether through entrepreneurship, employment, or investment, wealth is generated through interactions with others, who contribute their skills, labor, and resources to create value and drive economic growth. In this sense, wealth creation is a collaborative endeavour, in which everyone plays a role in contributing to the prosperity of the whole.

The Importance of Giving Back

As beneficiaries of society's collective efforts, we have a moral and ethical responsibility to give back—to reinvest our wealth and resources in ways that benefit others and contribute to the common good. This can take many forms, from philanthropy and charitable giving to employee benefits and community development initiatives. By giving back to society and our teams, we not only fulfil our obligations as responsible members of society but also create a more equitable and sustainable future for all.

Beyond Charity: Taking Care of Everyone

Giving back is not just about writing a check or making a donation—it's about taking care of everyone we come across with the resources and opportunities available to us. This may involve providing fair wages and benefits to our employees, investing in training and development programs to support their growth and advancement, or creating a positive work environment that fosters collaboration, creativity, and well-being. It may also involve supporting local businesses, suppliers, and communities through responsible sourcing, fair trade practices, and community engagement initiatives.

The Power of Collective Impact

When we give back to society and our teams, we create a ripple effect of positive impact that extends far beyond our immediate sphere of influence. By investing in education, healthcare, and infrastructure, we empower individuals and communities to thrive and prosper, laying the foundation for a brighter and more prosperous future for all. Through collective action and collaboration, we harness the power of wealth to address pressing social and environmental challenges, creating a world that is more just, equitable, and sustainable for future generations.

Completing the circle of wealth

Completing the circle of wealth is about more than just making money—it's about using our wealth and resources to make a positive difference in the world. By giving back to society and our teams, we create a sustainable ecosystem of growth and prosperity that benefits everyone involved. Whether through philanthropy, employee benefits, or community development initiatives, we have the power to create a brighter future for all by reinvesting our wealth in ways that uplift and empower others. In doing so, we not only fulfil our moral and ethical obligations as responsible members of society but also create a legacy of impact and inspiration that transcends generations.

Spiritual Wisdom: The Path to Clarity and Prosperity

In the quest for clarity of thought and purposeful work, many turn to spiritual teachings for guidance and inspiration. Spiritual wisdom offers a unique perspective on the nature of reality, human consciousness, and the pursuit of prosperity. By learning from spiritual teachers who have mastered the art of attracting wealth through clarity of thought, we gain insights and practices that can transform our lives and elevate our work to new heights of success and fulfilment.

Understanding Clarity of Thought

Clarity of thought is a state of mind characterised by focus, coherence, and alignment with one's highest intentions and values. It is the ability to discern truth from illusion, wisdom from ignorance, and purpose from distraction. In the realm of spirituality, clarity of thought is cultivated through practices such as meditation, mindfulness, and self-inquiry, which quiet the mind, deepen awareness, and connect us to the deeper truths of existence.

The Spiritual Path to Prosperity

Spiritual teachings often emphasise the importance of aligning our thoughts, beliefs, and intentions with our highest aspirations and values. By cultivating clarity of thought and intention, we create a powerful energetic resonance that attracts abundance and prosperity into our lives. Spiritual teachers who have mastered this art demonstrate how clarity of thought can manifest in tangible results, such as financial success, professional achievement, and personal fulfilment.

Learning from Spiritual Teachers

By studying the lives and teachings of spiritual teachers who have achieved wealth and success through clarity of thought, we gain valuable insights and practices that can help us on our own journey of prosperity. These teachers offer wisdom and guidance on how to align our thoughts, beliefs, and intentions with our highest aspirations and values, creating a fertile ground for abundance to flourish. Through their example, we witness firsthand the transformative power of clarity of thought in attracting wealth and prosperity into our lives.

Practices for Cultivating Clarity

To cultivate clarity of thought and attract wealth into our lives, spiritual teachings offer a variety of practices and techniques. These may include:

Meditation: Quieting the mind and deepening awareness through meditation helps to cultivate clarity of thought and align with the flow of abundance.

Visualisation: Using the power of imagination and visualisation to clarify goals, intentions, and desires, creating a clear mental image of the desired outcome.

Affirmations: Affirming positive beliefs and intentions helps to reprogram the subconscious mind and align with the energy of abundance.

Gratitude: Cultivating an attitude of gratitude for the abundance that already exists in our lives helps to shift our focus from lack to abundance, attracting more blessings into our lives.

Being spiritual means bringing clarity of thought and work into every aspect of our lives. By learning from spiritual teachers who have mastered the art of attracting wealth through clarity of thought, we gain valuable insights and practices that can transform our lives and elevate our work to new heights of success and fulfilment. Through practices such as meditation, visualisation, affirmations, and gratitude, we align our thoughts, beliefs, and intentions with our highest aspirations and values, creating a fertile ground for abundance to flourish. In doing so, we unlock the transformative power of clarity of thought in attracting wealth and prosperity into our lives.

Fostering a Spiritual Bond Among Teams

In the dynamic landscape of modern workplaces, fostering a sense of unity and connection among team members is crucial for achieving collective success and fulfilment. While traditional team-building activities may focus on productivity and efficiency, creating a spiritual bond among team members goes deeper—it cultivates a sense of shared purpose, empathy, and trust that transcends individual differences and fosters a culture of collaboration, creativity, and well-being. By embracing spiritual principles and practices, teams can forge a deeper connection with one another, tap into their collective wisdom and potential, and create a supportive and harmonious work environment where everyone thrives.

Understanding the Spiritual Bond

A spiritual bond among team members is rooted in a sense of interconnectedness and shared humanity. It is about recognising and honouring the divine spark within each individual, and fostering a culture of empathy, compassion, and mutual respect. This bond transcends traditional notions of hierarchy and competition, and fosters a sense of unity and collaboration that enables teams to overcome challenges, innovate, and achieve their goals with greater ease and grace.

Cultivating Spiritual Principles

Creating a spiritual bond among team members begins with cultivating spiritual principles such as presence, authenticity, and compassion in the workplace. This involves creating space for open and honest communication, actively listening to one another's perspectives, and practicing empathy and understanding in all interactions. By fostering a culture of inclusivity and acceptance, teams can create an environment where everyone feels valued, respected, and supported.

Practicing Mindfulness and Meditation

Mindfulness and meditation are powerful tools for cultivating a spiritual bond among team members. By practicing mindfulness together, teams can cultivate a sense of presence and awareness that deepens their connection with one another and fosters a greater sense of unity and purpose. Meditation practices such as loving-kindness meditation can also help teams cultivate feelings of compassion and goodwill towards one another, strengthening their bond and creating a supportive and harmonious work environment.

Fostering Collaboration and Creativity

A spiritual bond among team members fosters a culture of collaboration and creativity where everyone feels empowered to contribute their unique talents and perspectives. By embracing diversity and inclusion, teams can tap into the collective wisdom and potential of all members, sparking innovation and driving positive change. By fostering an environment where everyone feels valued and supported, teams can unleash their creativity and problem-solving abilities, leading to greater success and fulfillment for all.

Building Trust and Resilience

Trust is the foundation of any successful team, and cultivating a spiritual bond among team members is key to building trust and resilience in the face of challenges. By fostering open and honest communication, practicing empathy and understanding, and supporting one another through difficult times, teams can build a strong foundation of trust that enables them to navigate obstacles and setbacks with grace and resilience.

Creating a spiritual bond among team members is essential for fostering a culture of collaboration, creativity, and well-being in the workplace. By embracing spiritual principles and practices such as presence, authenticity, and compassion, teams can cultivate a sense of unity and connection that enables them to achieve their goals with greater ease and grace.

By fostering a culture of inclusivity and acceptance, practicing mindfulness and meditation, fostering collaboration and creativity, and building trust and resilience, teams can create a supportive and harmonious work environment where everyone thrives.

Harnessing Spirituality to Build Collective Intelligence

In the journey towards collective intelligence—a synergy of wisdom, creativity, and innovation—spirituality emerges as a powerful catalyst, offering insights and practices that transcend the limitations of individual intellect and ego. By embracing spiritual principles such as presence, empathy, and interconnectedness, teams and communities can tap into a deeper reservoir of wisdom and insight, unlocking the full potential of collective intelligence to solve complex problems, foster innovation, and create positive change in the world.

The Essence of Collective Intelligence

Collective intelligence is more than just the sum of individual intellects—it is a dynamic synergy that arises when diverse perspectives, experiences, and talents come together in pursuit of a common goal. It is about harnessing the collective wisdom and creativity of a group to achieve outcomes that surpass what any individual could accomplish alone. At its core, collective intelligence is rooted in openness, collaboration, and a shared commitment to learning and growth.

Spirituality as a Catalyst for Collective Intelligence

Spirituality offers a unique lens through which to cultivate collective intelligence, drawing on timeless wisdom traditions and practices that honor the interconnectedness of all beings and the inherent divinity within each individual. By embracing spiritual principles such as presence, mindfulness, and compassion, teams and communities can create an environment where everyone feels valued, respected, and empowered to contribute their unique gifts and perspectives. This sense of connection and belonging fosters a culture of collaboration and trust, laying the foundation for collective intelligence to flourish.

Practices for Cultivating Collective Intelligence

There are many practices rooted in spirituality that can help teams and communities cultivate collective intelligence:

1. **Mindfulness and Presence:** By practicing mindfulness and presence, teams can cultivate a deeper awareness of themselves and their surroundings, enabling them to stay grounded and focused amidst the complexities of collaborative work.
2. **Empathy and Understanding:** By practicing empathy and understanding, teams can create a culture of inclusivity and acceptance, where everyone feels heard, valued, and respected.
3. **Active Listening and Dialogue:** By engaging in active listening and dialogue, teams can foster open and honest communication, allowing diverse perspectives to be heard and integrated into decision-making processes.
4. **Collaborative Problem-Solving:** By approaching challenges with a spirit of collaboration and cooperation, teams can tap into the collective wisdom and creativity of the group, leading to innovative solutions that surpass what any individual could achieve alone.
5. **Celebrating Diversity and Inclusion:** By celebrating diversity and inclusion, teams can create an environment where everyone feels welcome and empowered to contribute their unique talents and perspectives.

The Impact of Collective Intelligence

When teams and communities harness the power of collective intelligence, they become more adaptive, innovative, and resilient in the face of change and uncertainty. By drawing on the collective wisdom and creativity of the group, they are able to solve complex problems, make informed decisions, and create positive change in the world. Through collaboration, cooperation, and a shared commitment to learning and growth, they unlock the full potential of collective intelligence to shape a brighter and more sustainable future for all.

Spirituality offers a powerful framework for cultivating collective intelligence—a synergy of wisdom, creativity, and innovation that transcends the limitations of individual intellect and ego. By embracing spiritual principles such as presence, empathy, and interconnectedness, teams and communities can create an environment where everyone feels valued, respected, and empowered to contribute their unique gifts and perspectives. Through practices such as mindfulness, empathy, active listening, collaborative problem-solving, and celebrating diversity, they harness the transformative power of collective intelligence to solve complex problems, foster innovation, and create positive change in the world.

Meditation for Business: Navigating Growth and Overcoming Challenges

In the fast-paced world of business, the ability to identify growth areas, observe weak points, visualize potential threats, and find solutions is crucial for sustained success and resilience. Yet, amidst the hustle and bustle of daily operations, it's easy for business leaders to become complacent or overlook critical issues that could threaten their success. Meditation offers a powerful tool for sharpening awareness, cultivating clarity, and tapping into intuitive insights that can help business leaders navigate growth and overcome challenges with grace and wisdom.

The Pitfalls of Success

Many businesses experience a decline after reaching a peak point of success. This can often be attributed to a combination of factors, including complacency, overconfidence, and a lack of awareness about potential threats and weaknesses. As businesses grow and expand, they may become entrenched in their routines and processes, making it difficult to adapt to changing circumstances or anticipate future challenges. This can lead to a false sense of security and a failure to address critical issues before they escalate into larger problems.

The Role of Meditation

Meditation offers a unique opportunity for business leaders to step back from the hustle and bustle of daily operations and gain perspective on their business from a higher vantage point. By cultivating a regular meditation practice, business leaders can quiet the mind, deepen awareness, and tap into intuitive insights that may be obscured by the noise and distractions of everyday life. Through meditation, they can identify growth areas, observe weak points, visualize potential threats, and find creative solutions to complex challenges.

Identifying Growth Areas

During meditation, business leaders can reflect on their business with a sense of curiosity and openness, asking questions such as: What are our strengths and weaknesses? Where are the opportunities for growth and expansion? By quieting the mind and tuning into their intuition, they may uncover hidden opportunities or innovative ideas that have been overlooked in the busyness of daily life.

Leaders can identify areas that may be ripe for improvement or optimization by cultivating a non-judgmental awareness of their business practices and processes. They can also observe potential threats or challenges that may be looming on the horizon, allowing them to proactively address these issues before they escalate into larger problems.

Visualizing Threats and Finding Solutions

Through visualization techniques during meditation, business leaders can mentally simulate potential threats or challenges and explore possible solutions in a safe and controlled environment. Visualization of various scenarios and outcomes can develop contingency plans and strategies to mitigate risks and navigate uncertainty with confidence and resilience.

Avoiding Complacency and Overconfidence

One of the greatest benefits of meditation for business leaders is its ability to cultivate a sense of humility and awareness that guards against complacency and overconfidence. While regularly stepping back from the day-to-day demands of their business and connecting with their inner wisdom, leaders can remain vigilant and responsive to changing circumstances, ensuring that they continue to adapt and evolve in an ever-changing marketplace.

Meditation offers a powerful tool for business leaders to identify growth areas, observe weak points, visualize threats, and find creative solutions to complex challenges. By cultivating a regular meditation practice, leaders can quiet the mind, deepen awareness, and tap into intuitive insights that may be obscured by the noise and distractions of everyday life. Through meditation, they can avoid the pitfalls of success, remain vigilant and responsive to changing circumstances, and navigate growth with grace, wisdom, and resilience.

Work as Worship: The First Step to Meditative Growth

In the hustle and bustle of modern life, it's easy to view work as a means to an end—a necessary obligation to earn a living and support ourselves and our families. However, when we shift our perspective and approach work as a form of worship—a sacred offering of our time, energy, and talents—we unlock the transformative power of meditative growth. By infusing our work with mindfulness and intentionality, we create a pathway to personal and professional fulfilment, tapping into a deeper sense of purpose and connection that transcends the confines of the nine-to-five grind.

Redefining Work as Worship

At its core, the concept of "work as worship" is about imbuing our daily activities with a sense of sacredness and significance. It is about approaching our work with a spirit of devotion and dedication, recognizing that every task, no matter how mundane or routine, has the potential to be a source of spiritual growth and fulfillment. When we view our work as an opportunity to express our highest values and aspirations, we elevate our daily activities to the level of sacred ritual, honoring the divine spark within ourselves and others.

Cultivating Mindfulness in the Workplace

One of the key elements of practicing work as worship is cultivating mindfulness in the workplace. Mindfulness involves bringing our full attention and awareness to the present moment, without judgment or distraction. Through the medium of practicing mindfulness throughout our workday, we become more attuned to our thoughts, feelings, and actions, allowing us to respond to challenges with greater clarity, equanimity, and grace. Whether we're engaged in a complex project or performing a routine task, mindfulness enables us to infuse our work with a sense of purpose and presence, transforming even the most mundane activities into opportunities for growth and self-discovery.

Integrating Intentionality and Purpose

Another aspect of practicing work as worship is integrating intentionality and purpose into our daily activities. Intentionality involves aligning our actions with our deepest values and aspirations, ensuring that every task we undertake is infused with meaning and significance. On setting clear intentions and goals for our work, we create a roadmap for success and fulfillment, guiding us toward greater productivity, creativity, and satisfaction. Whether we're interacting with colleagues, serving customers, or tackling challenging projects, intentionality helps us stay focused on what truly matters, fostering a sense of purpose and fulfillment in everything we do.

Honoring the Spirit of Collaboration and Service

Practicing work as worship also involves honoring the spirit of collaboration and service in the workplace. Instead of viewing our colleagues as competitors or obstacles to our success, we recognize them as fellow travelers on the journey of life, each bringing their own unique gifts and perspectives to the table. By fostering a culture of cooperation, empathy, and mutual support, we create an environment where everyone feels valued, respected, and empowered to contribute their best work.

Whether we're leading a team, collaborating on a project, or serving customers, the spirit of collaboration and service reminds us that we are all interconnected and interdependent, working together towards a common purpose and vision.

Work as worship is not just a philosophical concept—it's a practical approach to finding meaning and fulfilment in our daily lives. Alongside approaching our work with mindfulness, intentionality, and reverence, we create a pathway to personal and professional growth that transcends the confines of the nine-to-five grind. Whether we're engaging in complex projects or performing routine tasks, work as worship reminds us that every moment is an opportunity to express our highest values and aspirations, honoring the divine spark within ourselves and others. In doing so, we tap into a deeper sense of purpose and connection that infuses our work with meaning and significance, transforming even the most mundane activities into sacred rituals of growth and self-discovery.

Meditating Growth: A Practical Guide

In the pursuit of personal and professional growth, meditation can serve as a powerful tool for fostering clarity, creativity, and insight. By incorporating meditation into our daily routine, we create space for introspection, observation, and reflection, allowing us to tap into our innate wisdom and potential. Here's a practical guide to meditating growth, designed to help you harness the power of mindfulness and visualization to unlock new levels of insight and innovation.

1. Setting the Stage for Meditation

Find a quiet and comfortable space where you can sit or lie down without distractions. Close your eyes and take a few deep breaths to center your thoughts and relax your body and mind. Settle into a comfortable position, whether it's sitting in a chair, on the ground, or lying down on your bed. Allow yourself to let go of any tension or stress you may be holding onto, and prepare to enter a state of deep relaxation and receptivity.

2. Visualizing the Brain Map

Begin by visualizing the brain map in your mind's eye. Imagine each area of your brain represented on the map, with different colors or symbols indicating strengths, weaknesses, and areas of potential growth. Take a few moments to observe the map with a sense of curiosity and openness, allowing your mind to make note of any patterns or insights that emerge.

3. Observing Strong Areas and Generating Ideas

As you visualize the brain map, pay special attention to the areas that represent your strengths and talents. Notice any patterns or themes that emerge, and allow yourself to reflect on how you can leverage these strengths to achieve your goals and aspirations. Be open to new ideas and insights that may arise, even if they initially seem unrelated or irrelevant.

4. Allowing Thoughts to Arise and Pass

During your meditation, you may find that your mind begins to wander or that irrelevant thoughts intrude upon your focus. Instead of trying to suppress these thoughts or force them out of your mind, simply observe them with a sense of detachment and let them pass. Remember that meditation is not about achieving a state of perfect concentration, but rather about cultivating awareness and acceptance of whatever arises in the present moment.

5. Continuing for 35 Minutes

Continue your meditation practice for 35 minutes, allowing yourself to sink deeper into a state of relaxation and receptivity with each passing moment. If distractions arise, gently bring your focus back to the visualization of the brain map and the observations you are making. Trust that the insights and ideas you are seeking will emerge in their own time, and allow yourself to surrender to the process without judgment or expectation.

6. Returning to Your Work

After completing your meditation, take a few moments to reorient yourself and ground your awareness in the present moment. Slowly open your eyes and take a few deep breaths, allowing yourself to fully integrate the insights and observations you have made during your practice. When you feel ready, return to your work with a sense of clarity, focus, and purpose.

7. Drawing a New Brain Map

Four hours after your meditation session, take some time to draw a new brain map, reflecting any insights or ideas that have emerged since your practice. Notice any shifts or changes in your perception of your strengths, weaknesses, and areas of potential growth, and allow yourself to make any adjustments or refinements to your goals and aspirations based on these insights.

8. Avoiding Immediate Corrections

Avoid the temptation to make corrections or changes to your plans immediately after your meditation session. Instead, give yourself time to sink into the insights and observations you have made, allowing them to percolate and integrate into your consciousness. Trust that the wisdom and guidance you have received will continue to unfold in the days and weeks ahead, guiding you toward greater clarity, creativity, and growth.

Meditating growth is a powerful practice that can help you unlock new levels of insight, creativity, and innovation in your personal and professional life. By incorporating mindfulness and visualization techniques into your daily routine, you create space for introspection, observation, and reflection, allowing you to tap into your innate wisdom and potential. By following this practical guide to meditating growth, you can harness the transformative power of meditation to cultivate clarity, creativity, and insight, leading to greater fulfillment and success in all areas of your life.

The Power of Friendship: Nurturing Spiritual Connections and Mutual Support

Friendship is a profound bond that enriches our lives in countless ways, offering companionship, support, and spiritual connection.
Drawing inspiration from the legendary friendship of Krishna and Sudama, we can learn valuable lessons about the transformative power of friendship and the importance of being a supportive friend in return.

The Spiritual Connection of Friendship

Friendship transcends mere companionship; it is a spiritual connection that nourishes the soul and uplifts the spirit. Just as Krishna and Sudama shared a deep bond of love and trust, our friendships too can serve as sources of guidance, inspiration, and mutual growth. When we open our hearts to genuine connections with others, we invite the divine presence into our lives, enriching our journey with wisdom and grace.

Embracing the Role of Sudama: Being Sudama

In the timeless tale of Krishna and Sudama, Sudama embodies the qualities of humility, devotion, and selflessness. As the devoted friend and confidant of Krishna, Sudama serves as a humble advisor and unwavering supporter. Similarly, we can strive to be like Sudama in our friendships, offering unconditional love, support, and guidance to those we hold dear. By nurturing our friendships with sincerity and compassion, we create a sacred space for mutual growth and spiritual connection.

Every Friend as Krishna: Embracing Guidance and Wisdom

In the story of Krishna and Sudama, Krishna assumes the role of the wise advisor and benevolent mentor. Likewise, Each friend in our lives plays the role of Krishna, offering valuable insights, counsel, and encouragement. By embracing the wisdom and guidance of our friends, we enrich our lives with diverse perspectives and shared experiences, empowering us to navigate life's challenges with grace and resilience.

Mutual Support and Empowerment

True friendship is a two-way street built on mutual support and empowerment. Just as Krishna and Sudama uplifted each other through their unwavering friendship, we too can empower our friends to reach their highest potential. Through celebration of their successes, comforting them in times of need, and offering a listening ear without judgment, we create a nurturing environment where growth and transformation flourish.

Being a Source of Strength and Comfort

In the journey of life, friends often serve as pillars of strength and comfort during times of adversity. Like Krishna, who supported Sudama through his trials and tribulations, we can offer our friends unwavering support and encouragement when they need it most. By being present, empathetic, and compassionate, we become beacons of light in each other's lives, guiding one another through the darkest of times.

Cultivating Deep Connections and Lasting Memories

Friendship is not just about shared experiences; it's about cultivating deep connections and creating lasting memories that transcend time and space. Just as Krishna and Sudama cherished their moments together, we too can cherish the bonds of friendship that enrich our lives. By investing time and effort into nurturing our friendships, we create a path of love, laughter, and shared experiences that endure forever in our hearts.

In conclusion, the story of Krishna and Sudama serves as a timeless reminder of the transformative power of friendship and the spiritual connections that bind us together.

By embracing the roles of Sudama and Krishna in our friendships, we cultivate a sacred space for mutual support, guidance, and growth.

Let us cherish the friends who walk alongside us on our journey, for they are the true treasures of our lives.

Nature operates on the principle of reciprocity: what you sow, you shall reap. Just as a farmer plants seeds with the expectation of a bountiful harvest, so too must we sow seeds of positivity, kindness, and gratitude in our lives. Trusting in the natural order of things means having faith that our actions will yield corresponding outcomes. Whether it's cultivating meaningful relationships, pursuing our passions, or striving for personal growth, the seeds we sow today will bear fruit tomorrow. By aligning our intentions with the rhythms of nature and trusting in the inherent wisdom of the universe, we can cultivate a life filled with abundance, fulfilment, and harmony.

Chapter 7: No False Ego

Ego can be a barrier to growth, clouding our judgment and hindering our progress. By embracing humility and authenticity, we pave the way for genuine self-improvement and advancement.

Embrace Your Expertise

In the vast history of human existence, each thread represents a unique skill, strength, or area of knowledge. To truly thrive in life, one must not only possess these qualities but also take pride in them. Your skill set is not just a collection of abilities; it's a testament to your journey, dedication, and potential to make a difference in the world.

Know Thyself

Before you can take pride in your skill set, you must first understand it. Take stock of your strengths, both innate and cultivated through experience. Reflect on your past achievements, the challenges you've overcome, and the knowledge you've gained along the way. Identify the areas where you excel and the passions that drive you forward. Knowing yourself is the first step towards embracing your expertise.

Cultivate Confidence

Confidence is the cornerstone of pride. Believe in your abilities and have faith in your potential to succeed. Understand that setbacks and failures are not reflections of your worth but rather opportunities for growth and learning. Cultivate a mindset of resilience, perseverance, and self-assurance. When you trust in yourself and your abilities, others will be inspired to do the same.

Celebrate Diversity

Just as no two individuals are alike, no two skill sets are identical. Embrace the diversity of talents and strengths that exist within yourself and others. Recognize that your unique combination of skills and experiences brings value to every situation. Celebrate the differences that make each person special, and seek opportunities to learn from those whose expertise differs from your own.

Strive for Excellence

Pride in your skill set does not mean complacency. Rather, it should inspire you to continually strive for excellence. Set ambitious goals, challenge yourself to push beyond your limits, and pursue opportunities for growth and development. Never settle for mediocrity when greatness is within your reach.

By continuously honing your skills and expanding your knowledge, you not only elevate yourself but also inspire others to do the same.

Share Your Wisdom

True pride in your skill set is not selfish; it's about sharing your gifts with the world. Be generous with your knowledge, skills, and expertise. Mentor others who are on their own journey of growth and self-discovery. Support and uplift those around you, knowing that your success is not diminished by the success of others. Similarly giving back to your community and empowering others to succeed, you create a ripple effect of positive change that extends far beyond yourself.

Your skill set is a treasure treasure of potential waiting to be unlocked. Embrace it, nurture it, and take pride in all that you have to offer. Know yourself, cultivate confidence, celebrate diversity, strive for excellence, and share your wisdom with the world. In doing so; you not only elevate yourself but also inspire others to reach new heights of achievement.

Embrace the Path of Lifelong Learning

In a world that is constantly evolving, the pursuit of knowledge is not merely a choice but a necessity for growth and adaptation. To thrive in today's dynamic landscape, one must embrace the mindset of lifelong learning—a journey without end, where each discovery leads to new horizons and deeper understanding.

The Curiosity Spark

At the heart of lifelong learning lies an insatiable curiosity—a thirst for knowledge that cannot be quenched. Cultivate this curiosity within yourself, and let it be the guiding force that propels you forward on your journey of discovery. Ask questions, seek answers, and never be satisfied with what you already know. The more you learn, the more you realize how much there is left to explore.

Embrace Change

The world is in a constant state of flux, with new technologies, ideas, and ways of thinking emerging every day. Embrace this change as an opportunity for growth rather than a source of fear or uncertainty. Stay flexible and open-minded, willing to adapt to new information and perspectives. Embracing change is not about abandoning what you know but rather expanding your understanding to encompass the ever-shifting landscape of human knowledge.

Seek Diverse Perspectives

True learning extends beyond the boundaries of your own experiences and beliefs. Seek out diverse perspectives and voices that challenge your assumptions and broaden your worldview. Engage in conversations with people from different backgrounds, cultures, and disciplines. Opening yourself up to new ideas and ways of thinking, you enrich your own learning journey and gain a deeper understanding of the world around you.

Learn From Failure

Failure is not the end of the road but rather a stepping stone on the path to success. Embrace your failures as opportunities for growth and learning. Analyze what went wrong, extract the lessons to be learned, and use them to inform your future actions. Remember that setbacks are not a reflection of your abilities but rather an inevitable part of the learning process. Embrace them with resilience and determination, knowing that each failure brings you one step closer to mastery.

Make Learning a Habit

Lifelong learning is not a one-time event but a habit to be cultivated and nurtured over time. Incorporate learning into your daily routine, whether it's through reading, listening to podcasts, attending workshops, or engaging in online courses. Set aside dedicated time for exploration and discovery, and make learning a priority in your life. The more you immerse yourself in the process of learning, the more natural and fulfilling it will become.

The journey of lifelong learning is not an easy one, but it is a deeply rewarding one. Embrace your curiosity, embrace change, seek out diverse perspectives, learn from failure, and make learning a habit. By doing so, you not only enrich your own life but also contribute to the collective knowledge and understanding of humanity. Remember that the path of learning is endless, but the rewards are limitless.

Embracing Authentic Ego

Ego, often vilified as a negative trait, can indeed be a double-edged sword. However, there exists a distinction between ego that is genuine and ego that is false. In the pursuit of excellence and authenticity in your work, a healthy ego can be a powerful tool—one that brings authority and authenticity to your endeavors.

Understanding Ego

Ego, in its simplest form, is the sense of self-esteem and self-importance that we all possess to some degree. It is the driving force behind our actions, motivations, and aspirations. While ego can sometimes manifest as arrogance or hubris, it can also be a source of confidence, conviction, and authenticity when harnessed correctly.

Authentic Ego vs. False Ego

The key distinction lies in the authenticity of one's ego. False ego is driven by insecurities, fears, and a desire for external validation. It often manifests as arrogance, defensiveness, and a need to prove oneself at the expense of others. In contrast, authentic ego arises from a deep sense of self-awareness, confidence, and conviction in one's abilities. It is grounded in authenticity, integrity, and a genuine desire to make a meaningful contribution.

The Power of Authenticity

Authentic ego brings a sense of authority and credibility to your work. When you believe in yourself and your abilities, others are more likely to trust and respect you. Authenticity shines through in everything you do, from the way you communicate to the quality of your work. It gives you the courage to take risks, pursue your passions, and stay true to your values, even in the face of adversity.

Balancing Confidence and Humility

While embracing authentic ego, it's essential to maintain a balance between confidence and humility. Confidence allows you to assert yourself and stand firm in your convictions, while humility keeps you grounded and open to feedback and growth. Recognize that you are not infallible and that there is always more to learn and improve upon. Embrace constructive criticism as an opportunity for growth rather than a threat to your ego.

Cultivating Authenticity

Authenticity is a journey of self-discovery and self-expression. Cultivate it by staying true to your values, passions, and unique perspective. Be genuine in your interactions with others, and let your authenticity shine through in your work. Trust in your instincts and intuition, and don't be afraid to let your true self be seen and heard. When you embrace your authentic ego, you bring depth, authority, and authenticity to everything you do.

Ego, when approached with authenticity and self-awareness, can be a powerful force for good.

Embrace your authentic ego as a source of confidence, authority, and authenticity in your work. Recognize the difference between authentic ego and false ego, and strive to cultivate humility alongside confidence. While embracing your true self and staying true to your values, you can harness the power of your authentic ego to achieve greatness in all your endeavors.

Distinguishing Between Ego and False Ego

In the realm of self-awareness and personal development, understanding the distinction between ego and false ego is crucial. While both concepts involve a sense of self, they manifest in vastly different ways and have profound implications for our interactions with ourselves and others.

Ego: The Core of Self

At its core, ego represents the sense of self, encompassing our beliefs, desires, and perceptions of identity. It is the lens through which we view ourselves and the world around us. Ego, in its purest form, is neither good nor bad—it simply is. It provides us with a sense of individuality and self-worth, motivating us to pursue our goals and aspirations.

False Ego: The Illusion of Self-Importance

False ego, on the other hand, is a distortion of the true self—a facade constructed from insecurities, fears, and a need for external validation. It is characterized by a sense of superiority, entitlement, and a need to prove oneself at the expense of others. False ego arises from a disconnect between who we truly are and who we believe we should be, leading to a cycle of comparison, competition, and self-doubt.

Key Differences

1. **Source of Validation:** The ego derives its validation from within, grounded in a healthy sense of self-worth and confidence. False ego seeks validation externally, relying on the opinions and perceptions of others to bolster its fragile sense of self-importance.
2. **Authenticity vs. Pretence:** Ego is authentic, reflecting our true beliefs, values, and aspirations. False ego is a facade, masking our insecurities and fears behind a veneer of arrogance and self-righteousness.
3. **Empowerment vs. Domination:** Ego empowers us to embrace our uniqueness and pursue our passions with confidence and conviction. False ego seeks to dominate and control, viewing others as threats to its sense of superiority.
4. **Connection vs. Isolation:** Ego fosters connection and collaboration, recognizing the inherent value and dignity of every individual. False ego fosters isolation and division, perpetuating a cycle of comparison, competition, and conflict.

Cultivating Authenticity

To transcend false ego and cultivate authenticity, we must embark on a journey of self-discovery and self-awareness. This journey involves embracing our vulnerabilities, acknowledging our insecurities, and learning to accept ourselves unconditionally. By reconnecting with our true selves and letting go of the need for external validation, we can reclaim our authenticity and live with greater purpose, meaning, and fulfillment.

Ego and false ego represent two sides of the same coin—the essence of self and the illusion of self-importance. By understanding the key differences between them, we can navigate the complexities of our inner world with clarity and insight. Embrace your ego as a source of empowerment and authenticity, and strive to transcend false ego by cultivating self-awareness, self-acceptance, and connection with yourself and others.

The Pitfalls of False Ego

In the theatre of life, our actions are constantly under the scrutiny of others. While a healthy ego can empower us to pursue our goals with confidence, false ego can be a perilous trap—one that distorts our judgment and leads us astray. Beware, for others are watching, and the facade of false ego may cloud your perception and your ability to make sound decisions.

The Allure of False Ego

False ego, with its veneer of self-importance and superiority, can be seductive. It promises validation, recognition, and a sense of control in a world filled with uncertainty and ambiguity. It feeds on our insecurities and fears, whispering tales of grandeur and success while masking the true essence of our being.

The Illusion of Invincibility

Under the influence of false ego, we may succumb to the illusion of invincibility—believing ourselves to be infallible and beyond reproach. We become blind to our shortcomings and deaf to the voices of reason that warn us of impending danger. Our judgment becomes clouded, and we make decisions based on arrogance rather than wisdom.

The Spectre of Misjudgment

Others, keen observers of human behavior, watch with a discerning eye as we parade our false ego for the world to see. They see through the facade, recognizing the insecurities and vulnerabilities that lie beneath. Their perception of us is colored by our actions, and they judge us not by the mask we wear but by the character we reveal.

The Importance of Authenticity

Authenticity, in contrast to false ego, shines through as a beacon of truth and integrity. It is the essence of our being, untainted by the need for validation or approval. When we embrace authenticity, we invite others into our world with open arms, fostering genuine connections based on trust, respect, and mutual understanding.

Navigating the Path to Authenticity

To navigate the treacherous waters of false ego, we must embark on a journey of self-discovery and self-awareness. This journey requires courage, humility, and a willingness to confront our deepest fears and insecurities. By peeling back the layers of false ego, we reveal the authentic self that lies beneath, a self, worthy of love, acceptance, and belonging.

Beware, for others are watching, and the mask of false ego may lead you astray. Embrace authenticity as your guiding light, and let go of the need for external validation or approval. By cultivating self-awareness, humility, and integrity, you can navigate the complexities of human interaction with clarity and grace. Remember, it is not the mask you wear but the character you reveal that truly defines who you are.

The Pitfalls of False Ego in Growth Planning

In the pursuit of personal and professional growth, a clear and well-defined plan is essential. However, when false ego takes the reins, what appears to be a path to success may instead lead to stagnation or even regression. Beware, for false ego may distort your perception and hinder your progress by wrongly calculating your growth plan.

The Deceptive Mirage of Success

False ego often paints a rosy picture of success, tempting us with promises of glory and achievement. It feeds on our desire for validation and recognition, urging us to pursue goals that are driven more by ego gratification than genuine passion or purpose. In our quest to prove ourselves to the world, we may overlook the true markers of growth and fulfilment.

Misguided Metrics of Progress

Under the influence of false ego, we may prioritize superficial metrics of success over meaningful indicators of growth. We measure our worth by external validation, such as accolades, titles, and material possessions, rather than the internal satisfaction that comes from personal growth and self-improvement. As a result, our growth plan becomes skewed, leading us down a path that ultimately fails to fulfil us.

The Danger of Complacency

False ego breeds complacency by fostering a sense of superiority and invincibility. We become so enamored with our perceived accomplishments that we stop pushing ourselves to grow and evolve. We rest on our laurels, believing ourselves to have reached the pinnacle of success, while in reality, we are stagnating and falling behind.

Resistance to Feedback and Change

One of the hallmarks of a false ego is resistance to feedback and constructive criticism. We become defensive in the face of dissenting opinions, unwilling to acknowledge our shortcomings or consider alternative perspectives. This closed-mindedness stifles our ability to learn and adapt, hindering our progress and limiting our potential for growth.

Cultivating Humility and Self-Awareness

To overcome the pitfalls of false ego in growth planning, we must cultivate humility and self-awareness. This requires a willingness to confront our insecurities and vulnerabilities, and to acknowledge that we don't have all the answers. By embracing a growth mindset and remaining open to feedback and new experiences, we can chart a course for growth that is authentic, meaningful, and sustainable.

Beware, for false ego may wrongly calculate your growth plan, leading you down a path of complacency and stagnation. To avoid this trap, cultivate humility, self-awareness, and a willingness to embrace change. Focus on meaningful indicators of growth and fulfillment, rather than superficial metrics of success. By doing so, you can chart a course for growth that is true to your authentic self and leads to lasting fulfillment and success.

Measuring Ego: A Quest for Realistic Evaluation

In the labyrinth of self-discovery, navigating the contours of one's ego can be a daunting task. Yet, to truly understand ourselves and our place in the world, we must embark on a journey of realistic evaluation—a journey that requires us to measure our ego with clarity and honesty.

Defining the Ego

Before we can measure our ego, we must first understand what it represents. The ego is the sum total of our sense of self—our beliefs, desires, fears, and perceptions of identity. It is neither inherently good nor bad but rather a complex interplay of thoughts, emotions, and experiences that shape our understanding of who we are.

Indicators of Ego

While the ego itself may be intangible, its manifestations are evident in our thoughts, behaviors, and interactions with others. Examining these manifestations, we can begin to measure the size and influence of our ego. Some indicators of ego include:

1. **Defensiveness:** How do we react when our beliefs or actions are challenged? Do we become defensive and resistant to feedback, or are we open-minded and willing to consider alternative perspectives?
2. **Need for Validation:** Do we seek external validation and approval to bolster our sense of self-worth? Are we overly concerned with how others perceive us, to the point where it affects our decisions and behavior?
3. **Comparison and Competition:** Do we constantly compare ourselves to others, measuring our worth based on their achievements and successes? Do we view life as a zero-sum game, where our success depends on others' failure?
4. **Humility and Gratitude:** How do we handle success and failure? Are we humble in victory and gracious in defeat, recognizing that both are part of the human experience? Do we express gratitude for the opportunities and blessings in our lives, rather than taking them for granted?

The Art of Realistic Evaluation

Measuring ego requires a delicate balance of self-reflection, introspection, and external feedback. It involves examining our thoughts and behaviors with honesty and humility, acknowledging both our strengths and weaknesses. Realistic evaluation is not about passing judgment or assigning blame but rather about gaining insight into ourselves and our patterns of behavior.

Tools for Measurement

There are several tools and techniques that can aid in measuring ego, including:

1. **Journaling:** Keeping a journal allows us to record our thoughts, emotions, and experiences, providing valuable insights into our patterns of behavior and areas for growth.
2. **Self-Assessment Surveys:** There are numerous self-assessment surveys and personality tests available that can help us gain a better understanding of our ego and its influence on our lives.
3. **Feedback from Others:** Seeking feedback from friends, family, and colleagues can provide valuable insights into how others perceive us and how our ego may be affecting our relationships and interactions.

Embracing Growth and Self-Improvement
Measuring ego is not a one-time endeavor but an ongoing process of self-discovery and self-awareness. It requires us to remain vigilant and open to feedback, willing to confront our ego with courage and humility. By embracing growth and self-improvement, we can cultivate a healthier relationship with our ego and navigate the complexities of human interaction with grace and authenticity.

Measuring ego is a journey of self-discovery—a quest for realistic evaluation that requires honesty, humility, and self-awareness. By examining our thoughts, behaviors, and interactions with others, we can gain insight into the size and influence of our ego and take steps toward cultivating a healthier relationship with ourselves and the world around us.

The Acid Test: Assessing Ego with Clarity of Thought
In the complex of the mind, the ego often lurks in the shadows, masking itself behind layers of complexity and deception. Yet, with the right tools and techniques, we can peel back the layers of illusion to reveal the truth beneath. One such tool is the acid test, a simple yet powerful method for assessing whether our ego is genuine or false.

Understanding the Acid Test
The acid test is based on the premise that genuine ego arises from a place of clarity and authenticity, while false ego is shrouded in confusion and illusion. By examining the clarity of our thoughts at layer three or four in the brain map—a metaphorical representation of our cognitive processes—we can gain insight into the nature of our ego and its influence on our perceptions and behaviors.

Layers Three and Four of Brain Map: The Nexus of Clarity
In the brain map, layers three and four represent the nexus of clarity—the point at which our thoughts coalesce into coherent patterns of understanding. At this level of consciousness, we are able to discern truth from falsehood, and reality from illusion. Our perceptions are untainted by the distortions of ego, allowing us to see the world with clarity and insight.

Assessing Clarity of Thought
To assess the clarity of our thoughts at layer three or four, we must engage in introspection and self-reflection. We must examine our beliefs, desires, and motivations with honesty and humility, questioning the assumptions and biases that shape our perceptions. By observing our thoughts without judgment or attachment, we can gain insight into the nature of our ego and its influence on our lives.

The Acid Test in Practice

The acid test is a simple yet profound exercise in self-awareness. To perform the test, take a moment to quiet your mind and observe your thoughts as they arise. Notice any patterns or themes that emerge, and pay attention to the clarity with which you perceive them. Are your thoughts clouded by confusion and uncertainty, or do they resonate with a sense of clarity and authenticity?

Interpreting the Results

If your thoughts exhibit clarity and coherence at layer three or four in the brain map, it suggests that your ego is genuine, that is, grounded in authenticity and self-awareness. Your perceptions are untainted by the distortions of false ego, allowing you to see the world with clarity and insight. Conversely, if your thoughts are mired in confusion and illusion, it may indicate that your ego is false—that is, driven by insecurities, fears, and a need for external validation.

The acid test provides a simple yet powerful method for assessing the nature of our ego and its influence on our perceptions and behaviors. Additionally examining the clarity of our thoughts at layer three or four in the brain map, we can gain insight into whether our ego is genuine or false. Armed with this knowledge, we can embark on a journey of self-discovery and self-awareness, freeing ourselves from the illusions of false ego and embracing the authenticity of our true selves.

Informed Opinions: The Antidote to Ego

In the noise of opinions that permeate our society, it's easy to fall prey to the allure of strong opinions—those bold declarations of belief and conviction that seem to demand attention and respect. Yet, behind the facade of certainty often lies the shadow of ego, masking our insecurities and fears with bravado and bluster. To transcend the trappings of ego and cultivate genuine understanding and insight, we must embrace the power of informed opinions—a journey of study, learning, and firsthand experience that leads to clarity and authenticity.

The Illusion of Certainty

Strong opinions, while often perceived as a sign of confidence and conviction, can also be a manifestation of ego. They stem from a desire to assert ourselves, to prove our worth and superiority in the eyes of others. Yet, beneath the surface of certainty lies a vast ocean of uncertainty—a recognition of our own limitations and the complexity of the world around us.

The Path to Informed Opinions

Informed opinions are not formed in a vacuum; they are the result of study, learning, and firsthand experience. Before we can make strong pronouncements on a subject, we must first immerse ourselves in its intricacies, seeking out diverse perspectives and viewpoints. We must approach our study with an open mind and a willingness to challenge our assumptions, allowing ourselves to be guided by evidence and reason rather than emotion or prejudice.

The Role of Learning

Learning is the cornerstone of informed opinions. It broadens our horizons, deepens our understanding, and empowers us to engage with complex issues in a meaningful and constructive way. Whether through formal education, self-directed study, or hands-on experience, learning allows us to transcend the limitations of ego and cultivate a deeper appreciation for the nuances and complexities of the world around us.

The Importance of Experience

While study and learning provide the foundation for informed opinions, firsthand experience adds depth and richness to our understanding. By immersing ourselves in the subject matter, whether through practical application or personal exploration, we gain insights that cannot be gleaned from books or lectures alone. Experience challenges us to confront our preconceptions and biases, forcing us to reevaluate our beliefs and assumptions in light of new information.

Embracing Humility

Informed opinions are grounded in humility—a recognition of our own fallibility and the limitations of our understanding. We must approach every subject with a sense of humility, acknowledging that our knowledge is finite and our perspectives are subjective. By embracing humility, we open ourselves up to the possibility of growth and learning, allowing us to engage with others in a spirit of openness and curiosity rather than arrogance or authoritarianism.

In the quest for understanding and insight, informed opinions serve as a beacon of clarity and authenticity. Through embracing study, learning, and firsthand experience, we can transcend the trappings of ego and cultivate a deeper understanding of the world around us. Armed with humility and curiosity, we can engage with complex issues in a meaningful and constructive way, fostering dialogue and understanding that transcends the limitations of ego and leads to genuine insight and understanding.

Mapping False Beliefs: Navigating the Terrain of Growth

In the labyrinth of the mind, our beliefs serve as guiding stars, illuminating the path we choose to traverse. Yet, not all beliefs are created equal, some lead us towards growth and understanding, while others tether us to the shadows of falsehood and stagnation. Thus, by using the brain map which is a metaphorical representation of our cognitive processes, we can navigate the terrain of growth and measure the alignment of our beliefs with our journey towards authenticity and self-discovery.

Understanding the Brain Map

The brain map is a conceptual tool that represents the various layers of our cognitive processes—from raw sensory input at the surface to abstract thought and insight at the core. At the surface level, our beliefs are shaped by external influences, such as culture, upbringing, and societal norms. As we delve deeper into the layers of the brain map, we encounter the nexus of clarity—the point at which our beliefs are distilled into coherent patterns of understanding.

Measuring False Beliefs

False beliefs, like shadows cast by the light of truth, lurk in the depths of the mind, distorting our perceptions and clouding our judgment. To measure the alignment of our beliefs with growth, we must examine their clarity and coherence at layer three or four in the brain map. Here, amidst the noise of external influences and internal biases, we can discern the truth from the illusion, separating genuine insight from the shadows of falsehood.

Belief: The Path of Growth

Beliefs, by their very nature, are neither right nor wrong; they are simply lenses through which we interpret the world. However, not all beliefs lead us towards growth and understanding. Those that are aligned with our journey towards authenticity and self-discovery resonate with a sense of clarity and coherence at layer three or four in the brain map. They empower us to transcend the limitations of ego and embrace new perspectives and ways of thinking.

Embracing Growth-Oriented Beliefs

Growth-oriented beliefs are grounded in humility, curiosity, and a willingness to challenge our assumptions. They foster an openness to new ideas and experiences, allowing us to engage with the world in a spirit of exploration and discovery.

By aligning his beliefs with growth, my friend navigates the terrain of the mind with clarity and purpose, transcending the shadows of falsehood and embracing the light of truth, and growth.

In the quest for authenticity and self-discovery, our beliefs serve as beacons of guidance and understanding. By using the brain map to measure the alignment of our beliefs with growth, we can navigate the complexities of the mind with clarity and purpose. Armed with humility and curiosity, we can transcend the shadows of falsehood and embrace the journey towards authenticity and self-discovery with clarity and purpose.

Belief: Igniting Growth in the Subconscious Mind

Belief, a potent force that courses through the veins of our subconscious mind, has the power to catalyze transformation and propel us towards our greatest aspirations. Like a spark igniting a flame, belief awakens dormant resources within us, unleashing the full potential of our being and guiding us along the path of growth and fulfillment.

Belief: The Catalyst for Change

Belief catalyzes change, transforming our thoughts, emotions, and actions into tangible manifestations of our deepest desires and aspirations. When we believe in ourselves and our potential to succeed, our subconscious mind mobilizes all resources at its disposal to bring our goals to fruition. It acts as a powerful ally, marshaling our inner strength and resilience to overcome obstacles and challenges on the growth path.

Harnessing the Power of Intention

Intention is the driving force behind belief, shaping our thoughts and actions in alignment with our goals and aspirations. When we set a clear intention and imbue it with unwavering belief, we send a powerful signal to our subconscious mind, activating its innate ability to manifest our desires into reality. By aligning our thoughts, emotions, and actions with our intentions, we harness the power of belief to create profound and lasting change in our lives.

Belief: Unleashing the Creative Force Within

Belief unlocks the creative force within us, unleashing our innate creativity and innovation to devise new solutions and possibilities. When we believe in our ability to overcome challenges and achieve our goals, we tap into a wellspring of inspiration and ingenuity that guides us towards novel and unexpected avenues of growth. Our subconscious mind becomes a fertile ground for exploration and experimentation, fostering the emergence of new ideas and insights that propel us towards our aspirations.

Belief: Cultivating a Growth Mindset

Belief is the cornerstone of a growth mindset, the foundation upon which we build our capacity for learning, resilience, and adaptability. When we approach life with a belief in our ability to grow and evolve, we embrace challenges as opportunities for learning and development. Our subconscious mind becomes attuned to the possibilities inherent in every experience, driving us to seek out new knowledge and skills that expand our horizons and propel us towards our goals.

Belief is a transformative force that ignites growth in the subconscious mind, driving us towards our greatest aspirations and unlocking the full potential of our being. By harnessing the power of belief, we tap into a wellspring of inspiration, creativity, and resilience that propels us towards profound and lasting change. With an unwavering belief in ourselves and our ability to succeed, we embark on a journey of growth and fulfillment, guided by the infinite possibilities that lie within us.

Brain Mapping Your Path to Genuine Self-Improvement

In the labyrinth of personal and professional development, the brain map serves as a guiding light, illuminating the pathways to growth and advancement. Charting the terrain of our cognitive processes, we gain valuable insights into the workings of our minds and unlock the keys to genuine self-improvement and advancement.

Understanding the Brain Map

The brain map is a metaphorical representation of our cognitive processes, ranging from surface-level sensory input to deeper layers of thought and insight. At the surface, our thoughts are shaped by external influences and societal norms, while deeper layers reflect our core beliefs, values, and aspirations. By examining the clarity and coherence of our thoughts at different layers of the brain map, we gain insight into the alignment of our beliefs and behaviors with our goals and aspirations.

Navigating Personal Growth

Personal growth begins with self-awareness—a deep understanding of who we are, what we value, and where we want to go in life. Through the medium of mapping the terrain of our cognitive processes, we gain clarity and insight into the patterns of thought and behavior that shape our lives. We identify areas for improvement and growth, setting clear intentions and goals that align with our values and aspirations. Armed with this knowledge, we embark on a journey of self-discovery and self-improvement, guided by the insights gleaned from the brain map.

Advancing Professionally

Professional advancement, like personal growth, begins with self-awareness and clarity of purpose. By mapping the terrain of our cognitive processes, we gain insight into the beliefs, attitudes, and behaviors that influence our professional success. We identify strengths to leverage and weaknesses to address, setting clear objectives and strategies for career advancement. Whether it's honing our skills, expanding our network, or seeking out new growth opportunities, the brain map serves as a valuable tool for navigating the complexities of the professional landscape and achieving our career goals.

Utilizing the Brain Map

The brain map is a versatile tool that can be used in a variety of ways to support genuine self-improvement and advancement. Whether through journaling, self-assessment surveys, or mindfulness practices, we can gain valuable insights into the workings of our minds and identify areas for growth and development. Thus, by regularly reflecting on our thoughts, behaviors, and experiences, we can track our progress, adjust our strategies, and stay focused on our goals. With the brain map as our guide, we unlock the keys to genuine self-improvement and advancement, both personally and professionally.

The brain map is a powerful tool for navigating the complexities of personal and professional development. By charting the terrain of our cognitive processes, we gain insight into the patterns of thought and behavior that shape our lives. With clarity and self-awareness as our guides, we embark on a journey of genuine self-improvement and advancement, unlocking our full potential and achieving our goals with confidence and purpose.

Lessons from History: The Downfall of False Ego

In the annals of history, tales of epic battles and legendary figures have captured the imagination of generations.

Among these stories, the Ravana, the formidable antagonist of the Hindu epic Ramayana, serves as a poignant reminder of the perils of false ego and its role in shaping the destinies of individuals and nations alike.

By delving into the depths of Ravana's character and his eventual downfall, we uncover timeless lessons about the dangers of false ego and the importance of humility, wisdom, and self-awareness.

The Rise of Ravana: A Tale of Ambition and Hubris

Ravana, the powerful demon king of Lanka, was renowned for his unparalleled strength, intellect, and ambition. Yet, beneath his facade of invincibility lay a deep-seated insecurity and arrogance—a false ego that blinded him to the consequences of his actions and clouded his judgment. Driven by a relentless desire for power and prestige, Ravana's ego propelled him into conflict with the gods themselves, setting the stage for his eventual downfall.

The Consequences of False Ego

Throughout the Ramayana, Ravana's false ego manifests in a series of reckless decisions and misguided actions that ultimately lead to his demise. His abduction of Sita, the wife of Lord Rama, and his refusal to heed the warnings of his advisers serve as stark reminders of the consequences of unchecked arrogance and pride. Despite his formidable capabilities and knowledge, Ravana's false ego blinds him to the wisdom of humility and the value of self-awareness, sealing his fate in the annals of history.

The Triumph of Humility and Self-Awareness

In contrast to Ravana's tragic demise, figures such as Lord Rama and Hanuman exemplify the virtues of humility, wisdom, and self-awareness. Lord Rama, with his unwavering devotion to dharma (righteousness) and his humility in victory, stands as a beacon of moral clarity and integrity. Hanuman, the devoted servant of Lord Rama, embodies the virtues of loyalty, courage, and selflessness, transcending the trappings of ego to serve a higher purpose.

Lessons for Today: Navigating the Path of Self-Discovery

The tale of Ravana serves as a timeless reminder of the dangers of false ego and the importance of humility, wisdom, and self-awareness in navigating the complexities of life. In a world filled with uncertainty and ambiguity, it is easy to succumb to the allure of ego and pride, but true greatness lies in embracing the virtues of humility, empathy, and self-reflection. By learning from the mistakes of history and cultivating a deep sense of self-awareness, we can chart a course toward genuine growth, fulfillment, and success, both personally and professionally.

The story of Ravana serves as a cautionary tale of the perils of false ego and the importance of humility, wisdom, and self-awareness in the journey of self-discovery and self-mastery. By embracing these timeless virtues and learning from the mistakes of the past, we can transcend the trappings of ego and chart a course towards genuine growth, fulfilment, and success in our lives.

Cultivating Humility and Wisdom

In the pursuit of expertise and mastery, it's easy to fall into the trap of arrogance and self-importance. However, true wisdom lies in recognizing the limits of our knowledge and embracing the virtues of humility, patience, and self-reflection. By adopting a mindset of humility and wisdom, we can navigate the complexities of life with grace and authenticity, fostering genuine connections and creating a positive impact through our actions.

Listening with Humility

Even when we are experts in a subject, there is always more to learn. Cultivating humility means approaching every interaction with an open mind and a willingness to listen and learn from others, regardless of their level of expertise. By humbling ourselves before the wealth of knowledge and experience that exists in the world, we expand our horizons and deepen our understanding of the complexities of our chosen field.

Patience in Expression

Strong opinions, while often fueled by passion and conviction, can also be a manifestation of ego. Taking the time to reflect before expressing a strong opinion allows us to consider alternative perspectives and weigh the consequences of our words. By cultivating patience in expression, we avoid the pitfalls of rash judgment and ensure that our contributions to the conversation are thoughtful, respectful, and informed.

Modelling the Way

True leadership is not about asserting dominance or proving oneself superior; it's about inspiring others through our actions and setting a positive example for those around us. By modeling humility, patience, and authenticity in our interactions, we create a culture of respect and collaboration that empowers others to do the same. Letting our work speak for itself allows our actions to be a testament to our expertise and integrity, fostering trust and admiration among our peers and colleagues.

Creating a Positive Ego through Work

Rather than seeking validation or approval through grandiose displays of ego, we can cultivate a positive sense of self-worth and confidence by allowing our work to speak for itself. By focusing on delivering excellence in everything we do, we build a reputation for reliability, integrity, and expertise that commands respect and admiration from others. Our accomplishments become a source of pride and satisfaction, reinforcing our sense of self-worth and contributing to a positive ego grounded in authenticity and humility.

Cultivating humility and wisdom is a lifelong journey—a quest for self-discovery and self-mastery that requires courage, patience, and self-reflection. By embracing humility in listening, patience in expression, and authenticity in action, we model the way for others and create a positive ego grounded in integrity and excellence. In doing so, we inspire those around us to do the same, fostering a culture of respect, collaboration, and growth that benefits us all.

Chapter 8: Build Team - You May Love People Without Liking Them

Effective teamwork is essential for achieving collective goals. This chapter explores the dynamics of building and leading teams, emphasizing the importance of collaboration, even in the face of personal differences.

In the realm of building teams, there exists a delicate balance between affection and affinity. It's not uncommon to find yourself in a position where you genuinely care for someone, yet struggle to connect with them on a personal level. This chapter delves into the complexities of forming cohesive teams, exploring the notion that love and liking are not always synonymous.

Understanding the Dynamics

At the heart of any team lies a diverse tapestry of individuals, each with their unique strengths, quirks, and idiosyncrasies. While it's natural to gravitate towards those whose personalities align with our own, effective team building demands a broader perspective. Recognizing that differences enrich the fabric of a team is the first step toward fostering an environment of inclusivity and collaboration.

Love vs. Like

Love, in the context of team dynamics, transcends mere personal fondness. It embodies a deep-seated respect for the inherent worth and potential of each team member. It manifests in empathy, support, and a commitment to their growth and well-being, irrespective of personal affinities.

Liking someone, on the other hand, pertains to the ease of interpersonal connection and shared interests. While likability can enhance camaraderie and cohesion within a team, it should not be the sole determinant of one's value or contribution.

Embracing Diversity

Teams thrive on diversity - of thought, background, and perspective. Embracing individuals who challenge our preconceptions and broaden our horizons is essential for innovation and progress. By valuing the unique attributes each team member brings to the table, we cultivate a culture of inclusivity and mutual respect.

Navigating Differences

Inevitably, conflicts and disagreements will arise within any team setting. How we navigate these differences speaks volumes about the strength of our collective resolve.

Approaching conflicts with empathy, open-mindedness, and a willingness to seek common ground fosters constructive dialogue and paves the way for meaningful resolution.

Building Bridges

Effective team building is akin to constructing a bridge - it requires a sturdy foundation, careful planning, and a shared commitment to reaching the other side. By recognizing the distinction between loving and liking, we empower ourselves to forge connections based on mutual respect and appreciation.

In the tapestry of team dynamics, love serves as the thread that binds us together, transcending individual differences and fostering a sense of belonging. While personal affinities may wax and wane, a steadfast commitment to each other's growth and success endures. Through embracing the diversity of thought and experience within our teams, we pave the way for collective excellence and enduring camaraderie.

Steps to Build a Team

Building a successful team is akin to crafting a masterpiece - it requires careful planning, attention to detail, and a collaborative spirit. In this chapter, we'll explore a step-by-step approach to assembling and nurturing high-performing teams that thrive in any environment.

Step 1: Define Your Objectives

Before embarking on the journey of team building, it's crucial to define clear objectives and outcomes. What are you hoping to achieve through this team? Whether it's launching a new product, solving a complex problem, or fostering innovation, clarifying your goals sets the stage for success.

Step 2: Identify Key Roles and Skills

Once you've established your objectives, identify the key roles and skills required to accomplish them. Consider the strengths, expertise, and experience needed for each position within the team. Strive for a balance of skills and perspectives to ensure comprehensive coverage of tasks and challenges.

Step 3: Recruit Diverse Talent

Diversity is the lifeblood of effective teams. Seek out individuals with a range of backgrounds, experiences, and perspectives. Embrace diversity of thought, culture, and expertise to foster creativity, innovation, and adaptability within your team.

Step 4: Establish Clear Communication Channels
Effective communication is the cornerstone of successful teamwork. Establish clear channels for sharing information, ideas, and feedback within your team. Encourage open dialogue, active listening, and transparency to foster trust and collaboration.

Step 5: Set Clear Expectations
Define clear roles, responsibilities, and expectations for each team member from the outset. Establish measurable goals and milestones to track progress and ensure accountability. By setting clear expectations, you empower your team to work towards a common purpose with clarity and focus.

Step 6: Foster a Culture of Collaboration
Create an environment where collaboration flourishes. Encourage teamwork, knowledge sharing, and mutual support among team members. Celebrate successes, learn from failures, and cultivate a culture of continuous improvement and growth.

Step 7: Provide Resources and Support
Equip your team with the tools, resources, and support they need to succeed. Whether it's access to training, technology, or mentorship, invest in your team's development and well-being. Empower them to overcome challenges and seize opportunities with confidence.

Step 8: Foster Trust and Respect
Trust is the bedrock of effective teamwork. Lead by example, demonstrate integrity, and foster an environment of trust and respect among team members. Encourage vulnerability, empathy, and authenticity to build strong interpersonal connections and foster a sense of belonging.

Step 9: Encourage Innovation and Creativity
Empower your team to think outside the box, experiment, and take calculated risks. Encourage innovation, creativity, and a willingness to challenge the status quo. Provide opportunities for brainstorming, problem-solving, and ideation to unlock new perspectives and solutions.

Step 10: Celebrate Success and Learn from Failure
Finally, celebrate successes and milestones achieved by your team. Recognize individual contributions and collective achievements to reinforce a sense of accomplishment and motivation. Likewise, embrace failures as learning opportunities, encourage reflection, and iterate on strategies for improvement.

Building a high-performing team is a dynamic and iterative process that requires dedication, perseverance, and adaptability. By following these steps and fostering a culture of collaboration, trust, and innovation, you can assemble a team that excels in achieving its objectives and making a meaningful impact.

Growth is Driven by Teamwork

In the journey towards growth and success, the power of teamwork cannot be overstated. Whether in business, academia, sports, or any other domain, cohesive teams are the driving force behind innovation, productivity, and progress. This chapter explores the transformative impact of teamwork on individual and collective growth.

Synergy of Collective Effort

At its essence, teamwork harnesses the collective energy, expertise, and creativity of individuals towards a shared goal. Therefore by pooling together diverse perspectives, skills, and experiences, teams can tackle challenges with greater efficiency and effectiveness than any individual could alone.

When I meet many young researchers during my lectures on 'Building Patent ecosystem'. They always mention the synergy generated by collaborative effort amplifies productivity, fosters innovation, and accelerates progress.

Leveraging Complementary Strengths

Successful teams are comprised of individuals with complementary strengths and expertise. By leveraging the unique abilities of each team member, teams can overcome obstacles and capitalize on opportunities with agility and precision. Collaboration allows individuals to focus on their areas of expertise while benefiting from the support and insights of their teammates, resulting in holistic solutions that drive sustainable growth.

Cultivating a Culture of Collaboration

Central to the success of any team is a culture of collaboration, trust, and mutual respect. When team members feel valued, supported, and empowered to contribute their ideas and perspectives, they are more likely to fully engage in the team's endeavors. While fostering an environment where open communication, constructive feedback, and shared decision-making are encouraged, teams can unleash their full potential and achieve remarkable results.

Learning and Development

Teamwork provides fertile ground for individual learning and development.

Through collaboration and knowledge sharing, team members have the opportunity to expand their skill sets, broaden their perspectives, and cultivate new talents. Experiencing diverse viewpoints and approaches fosters intellectual curiosity, adaptability, and personal growth, enabling individuals to evolve into well-rounded professionals capable of navigating complex challenges with confidence.

Ability to recover in the Face of Adversity

Inevitably, teams will encounter obstacles, setbacks, and unforeseen challenges on their path to growth. However, it is in these moments of adversity that the true strength of teamwork shines. By rallying together, supporting one another, and leveraging collective expertise, teams can overcome adversity with resilience and determination. The bonds forged through shared struggles deepen trust and solidarity, fortifying the team's resolve and propelling them towards even greater heights of achievement.

Celebrating Shared Success

Ultimately, the journey of growth is not just about achieving individual milestones, but about celebrating shared success as a team. Recognizing and acknowledging the contributions of each team member fosters a sense of belonging, pride, and camaraderie. Hence celebrating achievements together, teams reinforce their collective identity and commitment to excellence, fueling a cycle of continuous improvement and success.

In the grand tapestry of human endeavor, growth is driven by the collaborative efforts of teams united in purpose and vision. Harnessing the power of teamwork, individuals can achieve feats beyond their wildest imagination, catalyzing transformative change and leaving an indelible mark on the world. As we embark on our journeys of growth and discovery, let us remember that together, we are truly unstoppable.

Fulfilling the Skills Gap through Team Collaboration

In an ever-evolving landscape of industries and technologies, the skills gap is a pervasive challenge faced by organizations worldwide. However, teams possess a unique ability to bridge this gap through collaboration, leveraging the diverse talents and expertise of their members. This chapter explores how teams can effectively address the skills gap and drive organizational success.

Identifying Skills Shortages

The first step in addressing the skills gap is to identify areas where the organization lacks the necessary expertise or competencies.

This may involve conducting skills assessments, analyzing performance metrics, and forecasting future needs. By pinpointing areas of weakness, teams can develop targeted strategies for skill development and acquisition.

Leveraging Collective Expertise

One of the greatest assets of teams is their collective expertise. By bringing together individuals with diverse backgrounds, experiences, and skill sets, teams can effectively address a wide range of challenges. Encouraging knowledge sharing, cross-training, and mentorship within the team enables members to learn from one another and fill skill gaps through collaboration.

Continuous Learning and Development

Teams should prioritize continuous learning and development as a cornerstone of their culture. This may involve providing access to training programs, workshops, and professional development opportunities. By investing in the growth and up-skill of their members, teams can ensure that they remain agile and adaptable in the face of evolving industry trends and technologies.

Strategic Recruitment and Onboarding

Strategic recruitment plays a crucial role in addressing the skills gap. Teams should seek out candidates who not only possess the required skills and expertise but also demonstrate a willingness to learn and grow. Effective onboarding processes are essential for integrating new members into the team seamlessly, providing them with the support and resources they need to succeed.

Collaborative Problem-Solving

When confronted with complex challenges that require specialized skills, teams can leverage collaborative problem-solving techniques to overcome obstacles. By breaking down silos and encouraging interdisciplinary collaboration, teams can harness the collective intelligence of their members to develop innovative solutions that address the root causes of the skills gap.

Agile Skill Development

In today's fast-paced business environment, agility is key to staying ahead of the curve. Teams should adopt agile methodologies for skill development, focusing on iterative learning, experimentation, and feedback. By embracing a growth mindset and embracing failure as a natural part of the learning process, teams can adapt quickly to changing circumstances and fill skill gaps more effectively.

Measuring Progress and Impact

Finally, teams should regularly assess their progress in addressing the skills gap and measure the impact of their efforts on organizational performance. This may involve tracking key performance indicators, soliciting feedback from stakeholders, and conducting periodic skills audits. By monitoring their success and course-correcting as needed, teams can ensure that they remain on track towards fulfilling the skills gap and driving organizational success.

Addressing the skills gap is a complex and multifaceted challenge that requires a concerted effort from organizations and teams alike. Leveraging the collective expertise of their members, prioritizing continuous learning and development, and embracing collaborative problem-solving, teams can play a crucial role in closing the skills gap and driving sustainable growth. As organizations continue to navigate the ever-changing landscape of the future, the ability to adapt, innovate, and thrive will be increasingly dependent on the collaborative efforts of skilled and empowered teams.

Unleashing the Wonders of Growth Through Teamwork

In the pursuit of growth, whether personal or professional, the power of teamwork is unparalleled. This chapter delves into how teams can act as catalysts for extraordinary growth, unlocking potential, fostering innovation, and achieving remarkable feats together.

Amplifying Individual Potential

Teams serve as incubators for individual growth and development, providing a supportive environment where members can thrive. By leveraging each other's strengths, expertise, and perspectives, team members can amplify their potential and achieve feats they never thought possible. Through collaboration and shared experiences, individuals are empowered to push beyond their limits and reach new heights of achievement.

Cultivating a Culture of Innovation

Innovation flourishes in the fertile soil of collaborative teams. By bringing together diverse minds and skill sets, teams can spark creativity, challenge assumptions, and explore new possibilities. Encouraging experimentation, risk-taking, and out-of-the-box thinking fosters a culture of innovation where groundbreaking ideas can take root, flourish and Patented. Through collective brainstorming, prototyping, and iteration, teams can turn visions into reality and drive transformative growth.

Driving Collective Impact

The true magic of teamwork lies in its ability to generate a collective impact far greater than the sum of its parts. When individuals unite around a shared vision and common purpose, they become a force to be reckoned with. By aligning their efforts, pooling their resources, and working towards a common goal, teams can achieve wonders that would be impossible to accomplish alone. Whether it's launching a new product, solving a complex problem, or driving organizational change, the collective power of teamwork can move mountains and create lasting impact.

Navigating Challenges with Ability to Recover

In the journey towards growth, challenges and setbacks are inevitable. However, it is in these moments of adversity that the strength of teamwork truly shines. Rallying together, supporting one another, and leveraging collective wisdom, teams can navigate obstacles with resilience and determination. The bonds forged through shared struggles deepen trust and solidarity, empowering teams to overcome even the most daunting challenges and emerge stronger than ever before.

Celebrating Shared Success

As teams journey towards growth, it's important to pause and celebrate the milestones along the way. Recognizing and acknowledging the contributions of each team member fosters a sense of camaraderie, pride, and accomplishment. Whether it's hitting a sales target, launching a successful project, or achieving a personal milestone, celebrating shared success reinforces the bonds of the team and fuels motivation for the journey ahead.

In the complex of human endeavor, the wonders of growth are woven by the collective efforts of empowered teams. Harnessing the power of collaboration, innovation, and resilience, teams can achieve extraordinary feats and leave an indelible mark on the world. As we embark on our own journeys of growth and transformation, let us remember the transformative power of teamwork and the limitless potential it holds to create a brighter future for all.

The Collective Intelligence of Teams: Many Bodies, One Brain

In the complex ecosystem of teamwork, the collective intelligence of a team serves as its guiding force, propelling it towards growth and success. This chapter explores how the metaphorical "brain map" of a team lead can align diverse thoughts and perspectives, simplifying complexities with clarity to hack growth effectively.

Understanding Collective Intelligence

Collective intelligence is the amalgamation of the knowledge, skills, and insights possessed by individual team members. Like neurons in the brain, each member contributes a unique perspective, forming connections and networks that enable the team to function as a cohesive unit. By tapping into this collective wisdom, teams can leverage their combined expertise to solve problems, generate ideas, and make informed decisions.

The Role of the Team Lead

Just as the brain relies on a central command center to coordinate its various functions, the team lead plays a critical role in orchestrating the efforts of the team. While providing vision, direction, and guidance, the team lead acts as the central hub around which the team's activities revolve. Their ability to synthesize diverse inputs, prioritize objectives, and communicate effectively is essential for aligning the team towards common goals.

Creating a Brain Map for the Team

A "brain map" for the team involves mapping out the collective knowledge, skills, and resources available within the team. This may include identifying individual strengths, areas of expertise, and potential gaps in knowledge. Thus by visualizing this information, the team lead can gain insights into the team's collective intelligence and identify opportunities for growth and development.

Aligning Thoughts and Perspectives

One of the primary functions of the team lead is to align the thoughts and perspectives of team members towards a common purpose. This involves fostering open communication, encouraging collaboration, and facilitating consensus-building. Creation of a shared understanding of goals, priorities, and expectations, the team lead helps to synchronize the efforts of individual team members and harness their collective intelligence more effectively.

Simplifying Complexity with Clarity

In the face of complexity, clarity is essential for driving growth and innovation. The team lead plays a crucial role in simplifying complex concepts, breaking down silos, and distilling information into actionable insights. Therefore it is observed that provision of clear direction, setting realistic goals, and defining measurable outcomes, the team lead empowers the team to focus its efforts and make informed decisions that drive progress.

Hacking Growth with Collective Intelligence

Harnessing the collective intelligence of the team allows for innovative approaches to hacking growth. By tapping into the diverse perspectives and expertise of team members, the team lead can identify new opportunities, anticipate challenges, and develop strategies for sustainable growth. Through continuous iteration, experimentation, and learning, the team can adapt and evolve in response to changing market dynamics and emerging trends.

In the interconnected world of teamwork, the collective intelligence of the team serves as its most valuable asset. By creating a brain map that aligns thoughts and perspectives, simplifies complexity with clarity, and hacks growth effectively, the team lead empowers the team to achieve remarkable feats and unlock its full potential. As we navigate the ever-changing landscape of the future, let us harness the power of collective intelligence to drive growth, innovation, and success.

The need for HR Management Skills in Driving Growth

In the dynamic landscape of modern organizations, effective human resource (HR) management skills are indispensable for fostering growth and success. This chapter explores how proficiency in HR management not only ensures the well-being and productivity of employees but also serves as a catalyst for organizational growth.

Strategic Workforce Planning

At the heart of HR management lies strategic workforce planning - the process of aligning human capital with organizational objectives. By forecasting future talent needs, identifying skill gaps, and developing recruitment and retention strategies, HR professionals ensure that the organization has the right people in the right roles at the right time. Strategic workforce planning lays the foundation for sustainable growth by optimizing the organization's human capital resources.

Talent Acquisition and Retention

A key aspect of HR management is talent acquisition and retention. Skilled HR professionals excel in attracting top talent, leveraging innovative recruitment strategies, and fostering a positive candidate experience. Moreover, they recognize the importance of employee engagement, career development, and work-life balance in retaining top performers.

Therefore by nurturing a culture of inclusivity, recognition, and growth opportunities, HR professionals cultivate a loyal and motivated workforce that drives organizational success.

Performance Management and Development.

HR management skills encompass the art of performance management and development. Effective HR professionals design performance appraisal systems, provide constructive feedback, and facilitate employee development plans. By setting clear expectations, recognizing achievements, and offering opportunities for skill enhancement, they empower employees to reach their full potential and contribute to organizational growth. Additionally, HR professionals play a pivotal role in identifying high-potential talent and nurturing future leaders through targeted development programs.

Employee Relations and Conflict Resolution

Maintaining positive employee relations and resolving conflicts are critical components of HR management. Skilled HR professionals excel in fostering a supportive work environment, promoting open communication, and addressing employee concerns promptly and fairly. By mediating conflicts, promoting diversity and inclusion, and upholding ethical standards, they cultivate a culture of trust and collaboration that fuels organizational growth.

Compliance and Risk Management

HR management also encompasses compliance with labor laws, regulations, and ethical standards. HR professionals ensure that the organization operates within legal frameworks, mitigates risks, and upholds ethical principles in all aspects of human resource management. Hence staying abreast of regulatory changes, implementing best practices, and conducting regular audits, they safeguard the organization's reputation and mitigate potential liabilities, paving the way for sustainable growth.

Leveraging Technology and Analytics

In the digital age, HR professionals leverage technology and analytics to enhance their effectiveness. From applicant tracking systems and performance management software to predictive analytics and data-driven decision-making, technology empowers HR professionals to streamline processes, gain insights into workforce trends, and make informed strategic decisions. By harnessing the power of data and technology, HR professionals optimize HR operations, drive efficiency, and support organizational growth.

With the help of a brain map, my friend's retail shop owner was able to visualize and analyze the common mistakes he had been making in managing his business and employees.

This cognitive tool revealed gaps in communication, recognition, and employee engagement that were contributing to high turnover rates. Motivated to improve, he acquired essential HR skills by reading several authoritative books on human resources management. These resources provided him with strategies for fostering a positive work environment, implementing effective training programs, and recognizing and rewarding employee achievements. As a result, he developed a more supportive and inclusive workplace culture, which significantly improved employee retention and satisfaction over the long term.

In today's growing business landscape, having good HR management skills is not just a luxury but a necessity for driving growth and success. Skilled HR professionals play a multifaceted role in strategic workforce planning, talent acquisition and retention, performance management and development, employee relations and conflict resolution, compliance and risk management, and leveraging technology and analytics. Investment in HR management capabilities, organizations can cultivate a thriving workplace culture, maximize the potential of their human capital, and achieve sustainable growth in the long term.

Chapter 9: Love is Key to Growth

At the heart of growth hacking lies love – love for oneself, for others, and for the journey itself. This chapter delves into the transformative power of love in fueling personal and professional growth.

Love: The Ultimate Driver for Growth

In the realm of personal and professional development, love emerges as a powerful force that propels individuals and organizations towards growth and success. This chapter delves into the transformative impact of love as a driving force, igniting passion, fostering connection, and inspiring greatness.

Love as a Catalyst for Passion

At its core, love infuses passion into our endeavors, fueling our drive to excel and pursue our dreams with unwavering determination. When we love what we do, we are willing to invest our time, energy, and resources wholeheartedly, transcending obstacles and pushing the boundaries of what is possible. Love ignites the spark that fuels innovation, creativity, and perseverance, propelling us towards personal and professional growth.

Love for Self: A Foundation for Growth

Self-love forms the cornerstone of personal growth and development. When we cultivate a deep sense of love and acceptance for ourselves, we unlock our full potential and embrace opportunities for growth with confidence and resilience. Love enables us to embrace our strengths, acknowledge our weaknesses, and embark on a journey of self-discovery and improvement. By nurturing a positive self-image and practicing self-care, we lay the foundation for holistic growth and well-being.

He had worked tirelessly to build his business, enduring years of relentless effort and sacrifice. Now, even as his business stands tall, he finds himself unable to take a break, gripped by the fear of losing everything he has built. This unyielding dedication has come at a steep cost: he has lost his sense of self-love and is stuck in a monotonous cycle, endlessly repeating the same tasks. In his fear-driven routine, he misses out on great opportunities to expand his horizons and explore new possibilities. His work, once fueled by passion and love, has become a prison, driven by anxiety and apprehension.

Love for Others: Fostering Connection and Collaboration

Love extends beyond ourselves to encompass our relationships with others. When we approach interactions with love, empathy, and compassion, we create a culture of trust, collaboration, and mutual support. By valuing the contributions and perspectives of others, we forge deep connections and cultivate a sense of belonging that empowers us to achieve collective goals and aspirations. Love fosters an environment where individuals feel seen, heard, and appreciated, unleashing the full potential of teams and organizations.

Love for family, friends, team, society, nature, spirituality, and wealth cultivates a mindset primed for growth hacking. This comprehensive love creates a powerful foundation for exponential growth, as it fosters a deep connection and appreciation for all aspects of life.

When you embrace everything around you with genuine affection, your perspective broadens, and you become more open to innovative ideas and opportunities. This holistic love fuels your drive, creativity, and resilience, enabling you to overcome challenges and achieve remarkable success. By nurturing these diverse relationships and passions, you unlock the potential for boundless growth and transformation.

Love for Purpose: Finding Meaning and Fulfilment

At the heart of growth lies a sense of purpose - a deeper calling that gives meaning and direction to our lives. When we align our actions with our values, passions, and aspirations, we tap into a reservoir of love that propels us towards our goals with unwavering commitment. Love for purpose fuels our perseverance in the face of challenges, sustains our motivation during times of adversity, and empowers us to make a meaningful impact on the world around us. By embracing our purpose with love and devotion, we unlock the key to sustained growth and fulfillment.

In the complex human experience, love emerges as the ultimate driver for growth - igniting passion, fostering connection, and inspiring greatness. Whether directed towards ourselves, others, or our purpose, love empowers us to transcend limitations, embrace opportunities, and achieve our full potential. As we navigate the journey of personal and professional growth, let us harness the transformative power of love to create a world where every individual and organisation thrives in the embrace of love's boundless possibilities.

Love What You Do or Do What You Love: Unveiling the Path to Fulfilment

In the pursuit of a fulfilling life and career, the age-old question arises: Should one love what they do, or do what they love? This chapter explores the nuances of this dilemma, uncovering the keys to finding purpose, passion, and fulfilment in both approaches.

Love What You Do: Finding Joy in Purpose

For many individuals, the path to fulfilment lies in finding joy and satisfaction in the work they do. By immersing themselves in their chosen field, embracing challenges, and cultivating a positive mindset, they uncover hidden gems of fulfilment in even the most mundane tasks. Love what you do advocates prioritize mastery, growth, and contribution, finding meaning and purpose in the impact they make through their work.

The Power of Purpose

At the heart of loving what you do is a deep sense of purpose - a driving force that imbues each task with significance and meaning. Whether it's serving others, making a difference in the world, or advancing a cause they believe in, individuals who love what they do find fulfilment in aligning their actions with their values and aspirations. Purpose infuses their work with passion, resilience, and a sense of direction that propels them towards greater heights of achievement.

Cultivating a Growth Mindset

Embracing a growth mindset is essential for those who love what they do. Rather than viewing challenges as obstacles, they see them as opportunities for learning and development. By embracing curiosity, resilience, and a willingness to step outside their comfort zone, they continuously expand their skills, knowledge, and capabilities. This growth mindset enables them to adapt to change, overcome setbacks, and thrive in dynamic environments, further enhancing their enjoyment and fulfilment in their work.

Do What You Love: Pursuing Passion and Authenticity

Alternatively, some individuals are drawn to the path of doing what they love - following their passions and interests wherever they may lead. By prioritizing authenticity, self-expression, and alignment with their values, they carve out a niche for themselves in pursuits that bring them joy and fulfilment. Do what you love advocates prioritize autonomy, creativity, and self-discovery, finding fulfilment in the freedom to pursue their passions on their own terms.

Embracing Risk and Uncertainty

Doing what you love often entails embracing risk and uncertainty, as individuals venture into uncharted territory in pursuit of their dreams. By cultivating a tolerance for ambiguity, embracing failure as a natural part of the learning process, and remaining resilient in the face of setbacks, they navigate the highs and lows of the entrepreneurial journey with courage and determination. This willingness to take risks and pursue their passions wholeheartedly is a testament to their commitment to living a life of purpose and authenticity.

Finding Balance and Integration

Ultimately, the choice between loving what you do and doing what you love is not binary but rather a spectrum, with opportunities for integration and balance.

Whether it's infusing elements of passion and purpose into one's current role, pursuing side projects and hobbies outside of work, or transitioning into a career that aligns more closely with one's passions, individuals can find fulfillment by blending elements of both approaches. Honoring their values, interests, and aspirations, they unlock the key to a life and career that is rich in meaning, joy, and fulfillment.

In the journey towards a fulfilling life and career, the conflict between loving what you do and doing what you love gives rise to a rich variety of possibilities. Whether one finds joy and purpose in their current pursuits or embarks on a quest to follow their passions, the key lies in aligning actions with values, cultivating resilience and authenticity, and embracing opportunities for growth and self-discovery along the way. As individuals navigate the complexities of this choice, may they find solace in the knowledge that the path to fulfillment is as unique and varied as they are, with boundless opportunities for joy, growth, and meaning awaiting those who dare to follow their hearts.

Redefining Our Relationship with Money: Love Money Like Breath

In our modern society, money often serves as a symbol of success, security, and status. However, the extent to which we prioritize and value money can vary greatly, influenced by factors such as upbringing, culture, and personal beliefs. This chapter explores the concept of loving money like breath, delving into the complexities of our relationship with wealth and the impact of upbringing on our attitudes towards money.

Understanding Our Relationship with Money

Money plays a multifaceted role in our lives, serving as a means of exchange, a measure of value, and a source of security. Our relationship with money is shaped by a myriad of factors, including our upbringing, experiences, and societal influences. For some, money represents freedom, opportunity, and abundance, while for others, it may evoke feelings of fear, scarcity, and anxiety.

Love Money Like Breath: Embracing Abundance Consciousness

The notion of loving money like breath challenges us to adopt an abundance mindset - a belief in the unlimited potential for wealth and prosperity in our lives. Rather than viewing money as a scarce resource to be hoarded or feared, we recognize it as a natural and essential aspect of our existence, flowing freely and abundantly into our lives. By embracing an abundance consciousness, we open ourselves up to greater opportunities for financial growth, fulfillment, and impact.

Unpacking the Influence of Upbringing

Our attitudes towards money are often deeply influenced by our upbringing and early experiences. The messages we receive from our parents, caregivers, and society at large shape our beliefs about money, success, and self-worth. Individuals who grow up in environments where money is perceived as scarce or taboo may develop limiting beliefs and fears around money, while those who are raised with an abundance mindset are more likely to embrace opportunities for wealth and prosperity.

Overcoming Limiting Beliefs

To love money like breath, we must first confront and overcome any limiting beliefs or negative associations we may have towards money. This may involve exploring our subconscious beliefs about wealth, examining the messages we received about money during childhood, and challenging any assumptions that no longer serve us. On reframing our thoughts and beliefs about money, we can cultivate a healthier and more empowering relationship with wealth.

Cultivating Financial Literacy and Empowerment

Financial literacy is essential for empowering individuals to make informed money decisions and achieve financial independence. On educating ourselves about budgeting, investing, and wealth-building strategies, we gain the knowledge and skills necessary to take control of our financial future. Moreover, by understanding the principles of abundance and prosperity, we can harness the power of money as a tool for personal and collective growth.

Integrating Love and Purpose into Financial Goals

Ultimately, loving money like breath entails aligning our financial goals and aspirations with our values, passions, and purpose. When we view money as a means to create positive change in the world, support our loved ones, and live a life of abundance and fulfillment, we infuse our financial journey with meaning and purpose. By integrating love and purpose into our relationship with money, we not only achieve greater financial success but also experience deeper levels of joy, fulfillment, and satisfaction in our lives.

In the varieties of human experience, our relationship with money is a reflection of our beliefs, values, and experiences. Thus by embracing the concept of loving money like breath, we shift our perspective from scarcity to abundance, from fear to empowerment. Through introspection, education, and alignment with our values and purpose, we can cultivate a healthier and more fulfilling relationship with money, one that empowers us to live lives of abundance, joy, and purpose

Embracing Wealth with Love: Declaring "I Love Wealth" with Pride

In our society, wealth often evokes a spectrum of emotions, ranging from admiration and aspiration to envy and suspicion. This chapter explores the transformative power of looking at wealth through the lens of love, boldly declaring "I love wealth" with pride, and embracing the potential for positive impact and abundance that it brings.

Redefining Our Relationship with Wealth

Our relationship with wealth is deeply intertwined with our beliefs, values, and experiences. Instead of viewing wealth through the lens of scarcity or fear, embracing it with love allows us to recognize its potential as a force for good in our lives and the world. We can shift from a mindset of lack to one of abundance by reframing our perspective, opening ourselves up to greater opportunities for growth, contribution, and fulfilment.

The Power of Affirmations

Affirmations are powerful tools for shaping our beliefs and attitudes towards wealth. By declaring "I love wealth" with pride and conviction, we affirm our commitment to embracing abundance and prosperity in our lives. Affirmations help to reprogram our subconscious mind, replacing limiting beliefs with empowering thoughts and opening the door to new possibilities and opportunities.

Embracing Abundance Consciousness

Love is the antidote to a scarcity mentality, opening our hearts and minds to the infinite possibilities of abundance. By embracing abundance consciousness, we recognize that wealth is not a finite resource to be hoarded or feared but a natural and essential aspect of our existence. With love as our guiding force, we attract greater prosperity into our lives and align ourselves with the flow of abundance in the universe.

Celebrating the Benefits of Wealth

Wealth, when used wisely, has the power to enrich our lives and the lives of others in countless ways. By acknowledging and celebrating the benefits of wealth, we honor its potential to create positive change and improve the quality of life for ourselves and future generations. Whether it's providing financial security, supporting loved ones, or investing in meaningful causes, wealth can be a source of joy, fulfillment, and purpose.

Leveraging Wealth for Good

With love as our compass, we can leverage our wealth to make a meaningful difference in the world. Whether through philanthropy, social entrepreneurship, or conscious consumerism, we have the opportunity to use our resources to address pressing social and environmental challenges and create a more equitable and sustainable future for all. Alignment of our actions with our values and passions, we can amplify our impact and leave a lasting legacy of positive change.

Overcoming Guilt and Shame

For some, the idea of loving wealth may evoke feelings of guilt or shame, particularly in a society that often equates wealth with greed or selfishness. However, by recognizing that wealth is simply a tool and that our intentions and actions determine its impact, we can release these limiting emotions and embrace wealth with love and gratitude. When we approach wealth from a place of love, we are empowered to use it as a force for good and create greater abundance and prosperity for ourselves and others.

In the journey towards a more abundant and fulfilling life, embracing wealth with love is a powerful act of self-empowerment and transformation. By declaring "I love wealth" with pride and conviction, we affirm our commitment to abundance, prosperity, and positive impact. With love as our guiding force, we can leverage our wealth to create meaningful change in the world and cultivate lives of joy, fulfillment, and purpose. As we embark on this journey, may we embrace wealth with open hearts and minds, knowing that by doing so, we unleash the full potential of abundance in our lives and the world.

The Essence of Love: Expecting Everything You Want for Yourself, for Others

In its purest form, love transcends self-interest and encompasses a deep sense of empathy, compassion, and generosity towards others. This chapter explores the profound concept of expecting everything you want for yourself and for others and the transformative power it holds in fostering connection, kindness, and collective well-being.

Love as Empathy and Compassion

At its core, love is rooted in empathy and compassion - the ability to understand and share in the experiences and emotions of others. When we expect everything we want for ourselves, and for others, we cultivate a deep sense of empathy that transcends individual desires and extends to the well-being of others. By recognizing the inherent worth and dignity of every person, we create a world where kindness, understanding, and compassion flourish.

Cultivating a Spirit of Generosity

Expecting everything we want for ourselves and others, involves cultivating a spirit of generosity and abundance. Rather than viewing resources, opportunities, or blessings as finite commodities to be hoarded or competed for, we recognize the infinite potential for abundance and prosperity for all. By sharing our blessings freely and supporting others in their journey towards success and fulfillment, we create a ripple effect of positivity and goodwill that enriches the lives of everyone around us.

Fostering Connection and Belonging

Love creates a sense of connection and belonging that transcends barriers of race, gender, religion, or nationality. When we expect everything we want for ourselves and others, we foster a deep sense of unity and solidarity that transcends individual differences. By embracing diversity, celebrating uniqueness, and treating others with kindness and respect, we create an inclusive and welcoming community where everyone feels valued, accepted, and supported.

Promoting Social Justice and Equity

Expecting everything we want for ourselves, and others compels us to advocate for social justice and equity. Therefore recognizing and addressing systemic injustices and inequalities that perpetuate discrimination, poverty, and marginalization, we strive to create a more just and equitable society for all. Love inspires us to stand up for the rights and dignity of others, to speak out against injustice, and to work towards creating a world where everyone has the opportunity to thrive.

Leading by Example

As leaders and role models in our communities, expecting everything we want for ourselves, and others is a powerful way to lead by example. By embodying the values of empathy, compassion, and generosity in our words and actions, we inspire others to do the same. Whether in our personal relationships, professional endeavors, or broader social movements, our commitment to love serves as a guiding light that illuminates the path towards a more compassionate and equitable world.

In a world often marked by division, strife, and inequality, love stands as a beacon of hope and transformation. By expecting everything we want for ourselves, and others we tap into the boundless power of empathy, compassion, and generosity to create a world where kindness, connection, and collective well-being thrive. As we navigate the complexities of human experience, may we embrace the transformative power of love and strive to create a world where everyone is valued, respected, and supported in their journey towards fulfillment and happiness.

Love's Manifestations: Sowing and Reaping the Benefits of Wealth

Love, in its multitude of forms, permeates every aspect of human experience, shaping our passions, pursuits, and professions. This chapter explores how individuals sow and reap the benefits of wealth by following their passions and embracing love in various domains of life, from production and sales to entrepreneurship and spirituality.

Love as the Essence of Nature

Nature is inherently abundant and generous, offering boundless opportunities for growth and prosperity. Love mirrors nature's abundance, inspiring individuals to cultivate their passions and pursue their dreams with unwavering dedication and enthusiasm.

By aligning their actions with their deepest desires and values, they sow the seeds of success and abundance, reaping the bountiful rewards that follow.

The Passionate Producer

One friend finds fulfillment in the art of production, immersing themselves in the intricacies of their craft on the shop floor.

With love as their driving force, they tirelessly manufacture thousands of products per day for a multinational corporation, finding joy and satisfaction in the tangible results of their labor.

Their commitment to excellence and attention to detail ensures the quality and efficiency of their work, earning them the respect and admiration of their colleagues and clients alike.

The Globetrotting Sales Enthusiast

Another friend's passion lies in the world of sales, where they embark on exhilarating journeys across the globe each year.

With a love for exploration and connection, they traverse continents and cultures, forging meaningful relationships and closing lucrative deals along the way.

Their charismatic personality and unwavering determination make them a force to be reckoned with in the competitive world of sales, as they embrace every opportunity to expand their horizons and achieve greater success.

The Digital Entrepreneur

For another friend, the allure of online sales beckons, as they harness the power of technology to carve out their niche in the digital marketplace.

With a love for innovation and entrepreneurship, they leverage their expertise and creativity to build a thriving e-commerce business, selling a myriad of goods on various online platforms.

Their keen eye for market trends and customer preferences ensures the success of their venture, as they delight in the thrill of seeing orders buzz in every minute.

The Risk-Taking Maverick

One friend thrives on the adrenaline rush of risk-taking, as they navigate the tumultuous waters of the stock market with fearless determination. With a love for challenge and adventure, he embraces the inherent uncertainty of the financial world, making bold decisions and reaping handsome rewards.

His shrewd instincts and calculated risks catapult them to success as a seasoned stockbroker, as they revel in the excitement of each new opportunity and conquest.

The Spiritual Guide

Lastly, one friend's love transcends material pursuits, as they dedicate their life to the pursuit of spirituality and enlightenment.

With love for wisdom and compassion, they share their insights and teachings with thousands of eager listeners, guiding them on the path towards a simple and spiritual life.

Their profound wisdom and gentle guidance inspire others to live with greater authenticity and purpose, as they sow the seeds of love and enlightenment in the hearts of all who seek their counsel.

In the vast medley of human experience, love manifests in countless forms, guiding individuals on unique journeys of passion, purpose, and prosperity. Whether in the realms of production, sales, entrepreneurship, finance, or spirituality, love catalyzes growth and fulfillment, empowering individuals to sow and reap the benefits of wealth in its many forms. As we navigate the complexities of life, may we embrace the transformative power of love in all its manifestations, cultivating a world where passion, purpose, and prosperity abound for all.

Love: The Unresolved Chemistry Between You and Work

In the intricate dance of life, love often finds its way into unexpected places, including the realm of work. This chapter delves into the enigmatic relationship between individuals and their work, exploring the profound and often unsolved chemistry that exists when love intersects with professional pursuits.

The Mystery of Work

Work, in its various forms, occupies a significant portion of our lives, shaping our identities, experiences, and aspirations. Like a complex equation waiting to be solved, work presents a crowd of challenges, opportunities, and emotions that stir the soul and ignite the imagination.

The mystery of work lies in its ability to evoke a spectrum of feelings, from passion and fulfilment to frustration and uncertainty, as individuals navigate the ever-changing landscape of their professional journey.

Love's Intriguing Presence

Amidst the hustle and bustle of the workplace, love quietly asserts its presence, weaving its way into the fabric of daily life. Love in the context of work is not always romantic in nature but rather encompasses a deep sense of connection, purpose, and resonance with one's chosen vocation. It is the intangible force that compels individuals to pour their heart and soul into their work, to pursue excellence with unwavering dedication, and to find joy and fulfilment in the pursuit of their professional endeavours.

The Quest for Compatibility

Just as in matters of the heart, compatibility plays a crucial role in the relationship between individuals and their work. When love and work are in harmony, there is a sense of alignment, resonance, and mutual enrichment that permeates every aspect of one's professional life. Individuals find themselves drawn to work that reflects their values, interests, and strengths, creating a symbiotic relationship that fosters growth, creativity, and fulfilment.

Navigating Challenges and Contradictions

Yet, the path to love and fulfilment in work is not always smooth or straightforward. Individuals may encounter obstacles, setbacks, and contradictions along the way, as they grapple with the demands of their profession and the complexities of their desires and aspirations. The unresolved chemistry between individuals and their work can give rise to feelings of uncertainty, dissatisfaction, and even disillusionment, as they wrestle with questions of meaning, purpose, and identity in the context of their professional lives.

Embracing the Journey

Despite the challenges, the journey towards love and fulfilment in work is a deeply rewarding and transformative experience. It is a journey of self-discovery, growth, and evolution, as individuals navigate the twists and turns of their professional path with courage, resilience, and an open heart. Along the way, they uncover hidden depths within themselves, forge meaningful connections with others, and discover new possibilities and opportunities for growth and fulfilment.

The Beauty of Unresolved Chemistry

In the end, the beauty of unresolved chemistry between individuals and their work lies in its inherent mystery and potential for discovery. Like a captivating puzzle waiting to be solved, work beckons individuals to explore, experiment, and uncover the hidden truths and treasures that lie within. It is a journey of exploration and self-expression, where love serves as the guiding force that propels individuals towards greater understanding, authenticity, and fulfillment in their professional lives.

As we navigate the intricate dance between love and work, may we embrace the enigmatic chemistry that binds us to our professional pursuits. Let us approach our work with an open heart and a curious mind, recognizing that love is not always neatly resolved but rather a dynamic and ever-evolving force that enriches and enlivens our journey through life. In the end, it is the unsolved chemistry between individuals and their work that makes the journey so fascinating, rewarding, and ultimately, deeply fulfilling.

Each Song as a Devotional Piece with Spiritual Love Connection

Each song listed is a devotional piece deeply imbued with spiritual significance, offering a pathway to connect with the divine across various religious traditions. From the serene recitations of the Hindu "Om Jai Jagdish Hare" to the soul-stirring notes of the Christian hymn "Amazing Grace," these songs provide worshippers with a means to express their faith and devotion. Islamic Nasheed like "Tala' al-Badru 'Alayna" and Sikh chants such as "Ek Onkar" serve as powerful reminders of spiritual truths and divine presence, fostering a sense of peace and reverence. Buddhist mantras like "Om Mani Padme Hum" and Christian prayers like "Ave Maria" encapsulate centuries of spiritual practice and devotion, each note and word resonating with historical and cultural depth. These songs, regardless of their religious origin, share a universal quality: they transcend the mundane, elevate the spirit, and offer solace and inspiration to believers, creating a sacred space where the divine and the human meet.

Music has long been a conduit for spiritual expression across cultures and religions. Each devotional song, with its unique melody and lyrics, serves as a bridge connecting the human soul with the divine. This explores the spiritual significance of devotional songs from various traditions, highlighting how these pieces transcend mere artistic expression to become profound acts of worship and connection.

Devotional songs across various religious traditions share a common purpose: to elevate the soul and connect with the divine love.

Whether through the meditative chants of Buddhism, the harmonious kirtans of Sikhism, the poignant hymns of Christianity, the soulful Nasheed of Islam, or the sacred bhajans of Hinduism, each song offers a unique pathway to spiritual connection.

These songs transcend cultural and linguistic barriers, uniting believers in a shared experience of devotion and reverence. Through their melodies and lyrics, they invite worshippers into a sacred space where the divine and human meet, fostering a profound and lasting spiritual connection.

Mapping Your Passion: The Brain's Blueprint for Achievement

In the intricate network of neural pathways that make up the human brain, lies a map of our deepest passions and aspirations. This chapter delves into the concept of the brain map, exploring how it serves as a compass guiding us towards what we love to do, and how harnessing its insights empowers us to make every effort to achieve our dreams.

Understanding the Brain Map

The brain map is a metaphorical representation of the neural connections and patterns of activity that occur in response to our thoughts, emotions, and experiences. It reflects our preferences, interests, and inclinations, providing valuable insights into what we love to do and what brings us joy and fulfillment. By analyzing the brain map, we gain a deeper understanding of our passions and aspirations, unlocking the key to unleashing our full potential and achieving our goals.

Identifying Your Passion Points

Within the vast expanse of the brain map lie clusters of neurons that correspond to our passions and interests. These passion points are activated when we engage in activities that align with our values, talents, and desires, triggering feelings of excitement, engagement, and flow. By identifying and nurturing these passion points, we can harness the power of our innate interests and strengths, paving the way for greater fulfilment and success in our personal and professional lives.

Pursuing Purposeful Action

Armed with insights from the brain map, we are empowered to take purposeful action towards achieving our goals. By aligning our actions with our passions and aspirations, we tap into a deep reservoir of motivation, focus, and determination that propels us towards success.

Whether it's pursuing a new career path, starting a passion project, or embarking on a personal journey of growth and self-discovery, the brain map serves as our guiding light, illuminating the path towards our dreams.

Overcoming Obstacles and Challenges

The journey towards achieving our dreams is not always smooth sailing. Along the way, we may encounter obstacles, setbacks, and moments of doubt that test our resolve and resilience. However, armed with the insights from our brain map, we can navigate these challenges with courage and determination. By staying true to our passions and remaining focused on our goals, we can overcome adversity and continue moving forward on the path towards success.

Cultivating a Growth Mindset

Central to the concept of the brain map is the idea of growth and development. Our passions and interests are not fixed but rather evolve and expand over time. By embracing a growth mindset, we recognize that failure and setbacks are natural parts of the learning process and opportunities for growth and self-improvement. With each challenge we overcome, we strengthen our neural connections, refine our skills, and deepen our understanding of what we love to do, ultimately bringing us closer to achieving our dreams.

In the intricate landscape of the brain, lies a treasure trove of insights into our deepest passions and aspirations. By mapping our brain's blueprint for achievement, we gain a deeper understanding of what we love to do and how we can make every effort to achieve our goals. Armed with this knowledge, we embark on a journey of self-discovery, growth, and fulfillment, empowered to pursue our dreams with passion, purpose, and unwavering determination. As we navigate the twists and turns of our personal and professional lives, may we always heed the guidance of our brain map, trusting in its wisdom to lead us towards a future filled with joy, success, and fulfilment.

Chapter 10: Forgiveness is a Driver for Growth Hacking

Forgiveness liberates us from the shackles of resentment and bitterness, opening the door to growth and renewal. In this chapter, we explore the profound impact of forgiveness on our journey towards self-actualization.

The First Step: Forgiving Yourself on the Path to Growth Hacking

In the pursuit of growth hacking, a journey marked by innovation, experimentation, and rapid iteration, the first and most crucial step is often the act of self-forgiveness. This chapter delves into the transformative power of forgiving oneself, exploring how it paves the way for personal and professional growth and unlocks the potential for success in the dynamic world of growth hacking.

Acknowledging Imperfection

To forgive oneself is to acknowledge one's imperfections, mistakes, and shortcomings with compassion and understanding. In the fast-paced environment of growth hacking, where success is often measured by the speed of execution and the ability to pivot in response to feedback, the pressure to perform flawlessly can be overwhelming. However, by embracing the reality of human fallibility and recognizing that mistakes are an inevitable part of the learning process, individuals can release themselves from the burden of self-judgment and cultivate a mindset of resilience and adaptability.

Letting Go of Past Failures

Forgiving oneself entails letting go of past failures and embracing the lessons they contain. In the world of growth hacking, where experimentation and risk-taking are essential for driving innovation and progress, failure is not only inevitable but often celebrated as a valuable learning experience. By reframing failure as an opportunity for growth and self-improvement, individuals can liberate themselves from the fear of making mistakes and instead approach challenges with confidence, curiosity, and a willingness to learn from both success and failure alike.

By letting go of the mistakes he made in overspending on online advertisements in the past, my friend is now ready to explore the opportunities in e-commerce once again.

It was a challenging journey for him, as accepting the financial loss required a significant amount of courage and resilience. However, this experience has made him wiser and more cautious.

He has learned valuable lessons about budget management and the importance of strategic planning. With a renewed sense of determination, he is prepared to apply these insights to navigate the e-commerce landscape more effectively.

Embracing Self-Compassion
Self-forgiveness is an act of self-compassion, rooted in kindness, empathy, and acceptance towards oneself. In the high-stakes environment of growth hacking, where intense pressure and competition can lead to burnout and exhaustion, self-compassion serves as a powerful antidote, nourishing the mind, body, and spirit.

By treating oneself with the same kindness and understanding that one would extend to a friend or loved one, individuals can cultivate a sense of inner peace, resilience, and well-being that fuels their creativity, productivity, and effectiveness as growth hackers.

Clearing the Path for Innovation
Forgiving oneself clears the path for innovation and creativity to flourish. In the fast-paced world of growth hacking, where bold ideas and unconventional approaches are often the key to success, self-doubt and self-criticism can stifle creativity and hinder progress. However, by letting go of the need for perfection and embracing a mindset of self-forgiveness, individuals can unleash their creative potential, explore new ideas with confidence, and push the boundaries of what is possible in pursuit of growth and innovation, Patents.

Empowering Growth and Resilience
Ultimately, self-forgiveness empowers individuals to embrace growth and resilience in the face of adversity. In the unpredictable landscape of growth hacking, where challenges and setbacks are inevitable, the ability to bounce back from failure and adapt to change is essential for success. By forgiving themselves for past mistakes and embracing a mindset of growth and resilience, individuals can harness the power of their experiences to fuel their journey towards mastery, innovation, and lasting success in the dynamic world of growth hacking.

In the quest for growth hacking, the first and most important step is often the act of self-forgiveness. By acknowledging imperfection, letting go of past failures, embracing self-compassion, and clearing the path for innovation, individuals can empower themselves to embrace growth and resilience in the face of adversity.

As they navigate the challenges and opportunities of the growth hacking journey, may they always remember the transformative power of self-forgiveness to unlock their full potential and achieve their goals with confidence, creativity, and unwavering determination.

Mastering the Art of Forgiveness: A Path to Healing and Growth
In the tapestry of human experience, forgiveness stands as a cornerstone of emotional well-being and personal growth. This chapter explores the profound art of forgiveness, delving into its transformative power to heal wounds, release burdens, and cultivate inner peace and resilience.

Understanding Forgiveness
Forgiveness is a complex and multifaceted process that involves letting go of resentment, anger, and bitterness towards oneself or others. It is not about condoning or excusing harmful behavior but rather about freeing oneself from the emotional burden of holding onto past grievances. At its core, forgiveness is an act of compassion, empathy, and self-love that opens the door to healing, reconciliation, and personal growth.

Embracing Self-Forgiveness
The journey of forgiveness begins with oneself. Self-forgiveness is the act of releasing oneself from the weight of guilt, shame, and self-blame that often accompany past mistakes or regrets. Acknowledgment of one's humanity, embracing imperfection, and treating oneself with kindness and compassion, individuals can free themselves from the cycle of self-criticism and self-judgment that inhibits personal growth and well-being. Self-forgiveness is a radical act of self-love that empowers individuals to embrace their worthiness and embrace their potential for growth and transformation.

Extending Forgiveness to Others
Forgiveness also involves extending compassion and understanding towards others who may have caused harm or hurt. It is a process of letting go of resentment and anger towards those who have wronged us, and choosing to release the hold that past grievances have on our hearts and minds. By practicing empathy, empathy, and forgiveness towards others, individuals can break free from the cycle of resentment and bitterness, and cultivate a sense of peace, acceptance, and connection with themselves and with others.

My friend in Shenzhen began forgiving his team's mistakes in manufacturing and focused on helping them learn from these errors. Instead of replacing them with a new team, he encouraged them to take new lessons from their past experiences.

This approach not only fostered a sense of trust and resilience within the team but also led to remarkable results. By emphasising growth and continuous improvement, he transformed his team's performance and achieved exceptional outcomes, proving that forgiveness, patience and guidance can be more effective than starting over with a new group.

The Healing Power of Forgiveness

Forgiveness has the power to heal wounds, mend broken relationships, and restore inner peace and harmony. Thus by releasing the emotional burdens of the past, individuals create space for healing, growth, and renewal in their lives. Forgiveness liberates individuals from the shackles of resentment and anger, allowing them to move forward with grace, resilience, and a renewed sense of purpose and vitality. It is a transformative process that opens the door to greater levels of joy, fulfillment, and connection in one's personal and interpersonal relationships.

Cultivating Forgiveness as a Practice

Forgiveness is not a one-time event, but rather an ongoing practice that requires commitment, patience, and self-awareness. It involves cultivating a mindset of compassion, empathy, and understanding towards oneself and others, and actively choosing forgiveness as a pathway to healing and growth. By integrating forgiveness into daily life, individuals can create a foundation of inner peace and resilience that supports them in navigating life's challenges and opportunities with grace and authenticity.

In the journey of life, forgiveness emerges as a powerful tool for healing, growth, and transformation. By mastering the art of forgiveness - both towards oneself and others - individuals can release the burdens of the past, cultivate inner peace and resilience, and embrace the fullness of their humanity with grace and compassion. As they navigate the complexities of human experience, may they always remember the transformative power of forgiveness to heal wounds, mend relationships, and illuminate the path towards greater levels of joy, fulfillment, and connection in their lives.

Steps to Forgiveness: A Pathway to Healing and Liberation

Forgiveness is a journey, a process that unfolds gradually as individuals navigate the complexities of their emotions and experiences. This chapter outlines practical steps to forgiveness, offering a roadmap for releasing the weight of past hurts and embracing a future filled with peace, compassion, and growth.

Step 1: Acknowledge the Pain

The first step towards forgiveness is acknowledging the pain and hurt caused by the actions of oneself or others. It's important to allow oneself to feel the full range of emotions that arise, whether it's anger, sadness, or betrayal. By confronting the pain head-on, individuals can begin to process their feelings and lay the groundwork for healing and transformation.

Step 2: Understand the Impact

Next, it's essential to gain clarity on the impact of the hurt and how it has affected one's life and well-being. Reflecting on the consequences of holding onto resentment and anger can motivate you to let go and move forward. Understanding the root causes of the hurt, whether it's misunderstanding, betrayal, or trauma, can also foster empathy and compassion towards oneself and others involved.

Step 3: Release Resentment

Forgiveness involves letting go of resentment and the desire for revenge or retribution. This doesn't mean condoning or excusing harmful behavior but rather freeing oneself from the emotional burden of holding onto anger and bitterness. Techniques such as journaling, meditation, or therapy can help individuals process their emotions and release negative energy, creating space for healing and growth.

Step 4: Practice Empathy and Compassion

Forgiveness is rooted in empathy and compassion, both towards oneself and others. Practicing empathy involves putting oneself in the shoes of the person who caused harm, understanding their perspective, and recognizing their humanity. Compassion involves extending kindness and understanding towards oneself and others, recognizing that everyone is deserving of forgiveness and redemption.

Step 5: Choose to Forgive

Forgiveness is ultimately a choice, a conscious decision to let go of the past and embrace a future filled with peace and freedom. It's important to remember that forgiveness is not a sign of weakness but rather a symbol of strength and resilience. By choosing to forgive, individuals reclaim their power and agency, releasing themselves from the grip of the past and opening the door to healing and transformation.

Step 6: Set Boundaries

Forgiveness doesn't always mean reconciling or re-establishing relationships with those who caused harm. Setting boundaries is an essential part of the forgiveness process, protecting oneself from further harm and ensuring that healing can take place in a safe and supportive environment. Boundaries may involve limiting contact with toxic individuals, seeking support from trusted friends or professionals, or engaging in self-care practices that promote healing and well-being.

Step 7: Cultivate Self-Compassion

Finally, forgiveness involves cultivating self-compassion and self-love, recognizing one's inherent worth and dignity as a human being. It's important to treat oneself with kindness and understanding, acknowledging that healing is a journey that takes time and patience. Practicing self-care, self-reflection, and self-acceptance can nurture a sense of inner peace and resilience, empowering individuals to embrace forgiveness as a pathway to liberation and wholeness.

Forgiveness is a transformative process that requires courage, patience, and self-awareness. On following these steps to forgiveness, individuals can release the weight of past hurts, cultivate inner peace and resilience, and embrace a future filled with compassion, connection, and growth. As they embark on this journey of healing and liberation, may they always remember that forgiveness is not only a gift to oneself but also a powerful force for healing and transformation in the world.

Forgiveness Acid Test: Igniting Growth through Self-Reflection and Adaptation

Forgiveness is a profound and transformative process that requires introspection, empathy, and a willingness to let go of past grievances. Just as individuals assess their alignment with their work or personal pursuits through the acid test, they can also apply this principle to the journey of forgiveness. This chapter explores the concept of the forgiveness acid test, emphasizing that if one doesn't sizzle with the process of forgiveness towards themselves or others, then they are ready for growth hacking in their emotional and spiritual journey.

She decided to forgive her cheating husband and move on, which significantly improved her professional performance.

For a long time, the emotional turmoil had consumed her thoughts, making it difficult to focus on her work. However, by letting go of the past and prioritizing her well-being, she managed to regain her concentration and drive. This shift in mindset allowed her to channel her energy into her career, ultimately becoming a successful businesswoman.

Her journey illustrates the power of forgiveness and the positive impact it can have on both personal and professional growth.

Understanding the Forgiveness Acid Test

The forgiveness acid test serves as a means for individuals to evaluate their readiness to embark on the journey of forgiveness. If one does not feel a sense of resonance, openness, or readiness to engage in the process of forgiveness towards oneself or others, it may indicate a need for introspection and adaptation. Just as in growth hacking, where innovation and agility are key, the forgiveness acid test provides a framework for individuals to assess their emotional and spiritual alignment and make adjustments as needed.

Signs of Readiness for Forgiveness

Several signs may indicate readiness for forgiveness, including a willingness to let go of resentment, anger, or bitterness towards oneself or others. Individuals may also experience a sense of inner peace, acceptance, or empathy as they contemplate the possibility of forgiveness. Additionally, a desire for healing, reconciliation, or growth may prompt individuals to explore forgiveness as a pathway to greater emotional well-being and spiritual fulfillment.

Embracing the Process of Forgiveness

When faced with the forgiveness acid test, individuals have the opportunity to embrace the process of forgiveness and cultivate a mindset of openness, compassion, and healing.

This may involve acknowledging past hurts or grievances, extending empathy and understanding towards oneself or others, and making a conscious choice to release the emotional burdens of the past. Embracing forgiveness as a pathway to growth and liberation, individuals can reclaim their power and agency, and embark on a journey of emotional and spiritual transformation.

Leveraging the Growth Mindset in Forgiveness

The forgiveness acid test is grounded in the growth mindset, a belief that individuals can develop and grow through effort, practice, and learning. By adopting a growth mindset towards forgiveness, individuals recognize that healing and reconciliation are ongoing processes that require patience, resilience, and self-reflection. They view forgiveness not as a destination, but as a journey of self-discovery and self-transformation, where each step brings them closer to greater emotional well-being and spiritual wholeness.

Cultivating Resilience and Adaptability in Forgiveness

Navigating the forgiveness acid test requires resilience and adaptability in the face of uncertainty and complexity. Individuals must be willing to confront difficult emotions, confront past hurts, and engage in honest self-reflection in order to move towards forgiveness. By cultivating resilience and adaptability, individuals can navigate the challenges and uncertainties of the forgiveness process with grace and courage, knowing that each step brings them closer to healing, reconciliation, and inner peace.

The forgiveness acid test serves as a powerful tool for individuals to assess their readiness to engage in the process of forgiveness and embrace new opportunities for emotional and spiritual growth. Therefore the recognizing the signs of readiness for forgiveness, individuals can leverage the power of self-reflection and adaptation to embark on a journey of healing, reconciliation, and inner transformation. As they navigate the complexities of the forgiveness process, may they always remember that forgiveness is not only a gift to oneself but also a powerful catalyst for growth, healing, and spiritual evolution.

Forgiveness: Embracing the True Blessing of Acknowledgment

Forgiveness is often described as a profound act of grace and liberation, offering individuals the opportunity to release the burdens of anger, resentment, and hurt that weigh heavy on their hearts. At the heart of forgiveness lies the acknowledgment of wrongdoing, whether it was done intentionally or inadvertently. This chapter explores forgiveness as a true blessing, emphasizing the importance of acknowledging all wrongdoings, whether they were committed with intent or ignorance.

The Power of Acknowledgment

Acknowledgment is the cornerstone of forgiveness, providing a foundation for healing, reconciliation, and growth. When individuals acknowledge their wrongdoing or the harm caused by others, they demonstrate a willingness to confront difficult truths and take responsibility for their actions. This act of acknowledgment is a powerful catalyst for transformation, opening the door to forgiveness and paving the way for healing and reconciliation to occur.

Intention Versus Ignorance

Wrongdoings can occur with varying degrees of intentionality. Some actions are carried out with full awareness and intent to cause harm, while others may be the result of ignorance, misunderstanding, or lack of awareness of the consequences of one's actions.

Regardless of the underlying motive, the impact of wrongdoing can be profound and far-reaching, leaving scars on the hearts and minds of those affected. Acknowledging all wrongdoings, whether they were committed with intent or ignorance, is essential for fostering healing, understanding, and reconciliation.

Compassion and Empathy

Forgiveness requires compassion and empathy towards oneself and others, recognizing the humanity and fallibility inherent in all individuals. By acknowledging the wrongdoings committed, individuals demonstrate empathy and understanding towards those who have caused harm, as well as towards themselves. This compassionate stance creates a space for healing and reconciliation to take place, allowing individuals to move forward with greater clarity, peace, and resilience.

Healing and Reconciliation

Acknowledgment sets the stage for healing and reconciliation to occur. When individuals acknowledge their wrongdoing or the harm caused by others, they create an opportunity for honest dialogue, understanding, and forgiveness to emerge. This process of healing and reconciliation is essential for repairing damaged relationships, restoring trust, and fostering a sense of unity and connection among individuals and communities.

Embracing Forgiveness as a True Blessing

In the journey of forgiveness, acknowledgment is a true blessing, offering individuals the opportunity to release the burdens of the past and embrace a future filled with peace, compassion, and growth. While acknowledging all wrongdoings, whether they were committed with intent or ignorance, individuals demonstrate a commitment to truth, integrity, and healing. This act of acknowledgment is a profound act of grace and liberation, empowering individuals to move forward with greater clarity, purpose, and resilience.

Forgiveness is a true blessing, offering individuals the opportunity to release the burdens of anger, resentment, and hurt that weigh heavy on their hearts. At the heart of forgiveness lies the acknowledgment of all wrongdoings, whether they were committed with intent or ignorance. By embracing acknowledgment as a catalyst for healing and reconciliation, individuals can pave the way for greater peace, compassion, and growth in their lives and in the world around them.

As they journey through the complexities of forgiveness, may they always remember the transformative power of acknowledgment to bring about healing, understanding, and reconciliation in their hearts and in the hearts of others.

Thank you: Harnessing the Power of Appreciation for Growth Hacking

In the fast-paced world of growth hacking, where innovation, experimentation, and adaptation are paramount, gratitude emerges as a powerful force for driving success and fostering growth. This chapter explores the transformative power of gratitude, emphasizing the importance of thanking everyone for their experiences as a valuable asset in the journey of growth hacking.

The Power of Appreciation

Gratitude is a potent tool for cultivating positivity, resilience, and connection in both personal and professional endeavors. When individuals express gratitude for their experiences, they acknowledge the value and significance of each encounter, whether it was positive or challenging. This act of appreciation creates a ripple effect of positivity, fostering a sense of abundance, fulfillment, and well-being in the lives of those who embrace it.

Learning from Every Experience

Every experience, whether it's a success or a setback, offers valuable lessons and insights for growth hacking. By expressing gratitude for their experiences, individuals acknowledge the wealth of knowledge, skills, and perspectives gained along the way. They recognize that each encounter, no matter how small or seemingly insignificant, contributes to their growth and evolution as growth hackers, propelling them towards greater success and innovation in their endeavors.

Building Relationships and Networks

Gratitude strengthens relationships and builds networks, fostering trust, loyalty, and collaboration among individuals and teams. When individuals express gratitude for the contributions of others, they affirm the value and importance of their efforts, creating a sense of belonging and appreciation within the community. This spirit of gratitude fosters a culture of generosity, reciprocity, and mutual support, where individuals are empowered to collaborate, innovate, and succeed together.

Cultivating Resilience and Optimism

Gratitude cultivates resilience and optimism in the face of challenges and adversity. When individuals express gratitude for their experiences, they shift their focus from what is lacking to what is present, fostering a sense of abundance and possibility. This positive mindset empowers individuals to navigate obstacles with grace and determination, knowing that every challenge is an opportunity for growth and learning.

Embracing Growth and Evolution

Gratitude for experiences is a catalyst for growth and evolution in both personal and professional domains. When individuals express gratitude for the lessons learned and the wisdom gained from their experiences, they embrace a mindset of continuous learning, adaptation, and innovation. This attitude of gratitude propels individuals towards greater success and fulfillment, inspiring them to push the boundaries of what is possible in their pursuit of growth hacking excellence.

In the dynamic world of growth hacking, gratitude emerges as a cornerstone of success and fulfillment. Expression of appreciation for their experiences, individuals harness the power of positivity, resilience, and collaboration to propel themselves towards greater innovation and success. As they navigate the complexities of the growth hacking journey, may they always remember to thank everyone for their experiences, knowing that each encounter adds value and richness to their lives and their endeavors.

Chapter 11: Growth Hacking - Truthfulness

Authenticity forms the bedrock of growth hacking. By embracing truthfulness in all our endeavors, we foster trust, integrity, and genuine progress.

Trust Yourself and All Resources: Cultivating Informed Trust in the Journey of Growth Hacking

In the dynamic realm of growth hacking, trust emerges as a cornerstone for success and innovation. However, blind faith can lead to pitfalls and setbacks. This chapter delves into the importance of trusting oneself and all available resources without falling into blind faith, emphasizing the need for informed trust to navigate the complexities of the growth hacking journey effectively.

The Pitfalls of Blind Faith

Blind faith, while seemingly reassuring, can lead individuals down a path of complacency and vulnerability. Relying solely on blind faith may result in overlooking potential risks, dismissing valuable feedback, or failing to adapt to changing circumstances. In the fast-paced environment of growth hacking, where agility and innovation are paramount, blind faith can hinder progress and impede the attainment of goals.

Informed Trust: The Foundation of Growth Hacking

In contrast to blind faith, informed trust is rooted in knowledge, discernment, and critical thinking. It involves evaluating one's capabilities, as well as the reliability and credibility of external resources, before placing trust in them. Informed trust empowers individuals to make informed decisions, take calculated risks, and leverage resources effectively in pursuit of growth hacking success.

Trusting Yourself: Self-Awareness and Confidence

Trusting oneself begins with self-awareness and confidence in one's abilities, intuition, and judgment. It requires a deep understanding of one's strengths, weaknesses, and values, as well as the willingness to take ownership of one's decisions and actions. By cultivating self-trust, individuals develop the resilience and adaptability needed to navigate the challenges and uncertainties of the growth hacking journey with clarity and conviction.

Trusting All Resources: Critical Evaluation and Collaboration

Trusting all available resources involves critical evaluation and collaboration with external sources of knowledge, expertise, and support. It requires discernment in assessing the credibility and reliability of information, as well as openness to diverse perspectives and experiences. By leveraging external resources judiciously, individuals can tap into a wealth of insights, ideas, and opportunities that drive innovation and growth in their endeavors.

Balancing Trust and Skepticism

Informed trust is a delicate balance between trust and skepticism, allowing individuals to embrace opportunities and take risks while remaining vigilant and discerning. It involves asking probing questions, seeking evidence-based solutions, and being open to feedback and constructive criticism. When this balance is maintained, individuals can navigate the complexities of the growth hacking journey with confidence, agility, and integrity.

In the journey of growth hacking, trust in oneself and all available resources is essential for success and innovation. However, blind faith can lead to pitfalls and setbacks. By cultivating informed trust rooted in self-awareness, critical evaluation, and collaboration, individuals can navigate the challenges and uncertainties of the growth hacking journey effectively. As they harness the power of informed trust, may they always remain vigilant and discerning, knowing that with a balanced approach, anything is possible in the dynamic world of growth hacking.

Faith as the Key Driver for Growth Hacking

Faith is a key driver for growth hacking, serving as the underlying force that propels individuals and organizations to pursue ambitious goals with unwavering determination. This deep-seated belief in potential and positive outcomes fosters resilience and creativity, essential traits for navigating the unpredictable terrain of growth hacking.

Faith fuels the confidence to take calculated risks, experiment with unconventional strategies, and persist through setbacks.

It also inspires trust and collaboration within teams, creating a supportive environment where innovative ideas can flourish. Ultimately, faith acts as a powerful catalyst, transforming vision into reality and driving exponential growth.

In the realm of growth hacking, where rapid experimentation and innovative strategies reign supreme, one often overlooked yet pivotal element is faith. This chapter delves into how faith acts as the key driver for growth hacking, underpinning the mindset and actions that lead to extraordinary growth.

The Foundation of Faith in Growth Hacking

Faith, in its essence, is the unwavering belief in the potential for success and positive outcomes. It transcends mere hope, embedding itself deeply into the psyche as a steadfast conviction. For growth hackers, this faith is not just a passive feeling but an active force that propels them forward. It is the belief that no matter how daunting the challenges, there is a path to success.

Building Integrity: Embrace Wholeheartedness in the Journey of Growth Hacking

In the pursuit of growth hacking excellence, integrity stands as a cornerstone, anchoring individuals in authenticity, accountability, and ethical conduct. This chapter delves into the importance of building integrity and avoiding half-hearted efforts, emphasizing the transformative power of wholeheartedness in driving success and fulfilment in the dynamic world of growth hacking.

The Essence of Integrity

Integrity is the alignment of thoughts, words, and actions with one's values, principles, and moral compass. It involves honesty, transparency, and consistency in all dealings, both personal and professional. At its core, integrity is about doing what is right, even when no one is watching, and upholding ethical standards and moral integrity in all endeavors.

Embracing Wholeheartedness

Wholeheartedness is the embodiment of integrity in action, reflecting a commitment to giving one's best effort and attention to every task, project, or endeavor. It involves showing up fully, with passion, purpose, and dedication, and embracing challenges with courage and enthusiasm. Wholeheartedness is the antidote to half-hearted efforts, infusing every action with authenticity, sincerity, and intentionality.

The Dangers of Half-Heartedness

Half-hearted efforts undermine integrity and dilute the impact of one's actions and contributions. When individuals approach tasks or projects with a lack of commitment or enthusiasm, they compromise their integrity and diminish their ability to achieve meaningful results. Half-heartedness breeds mediocrity which erodes trust and undermines credibility, hindering progress and impeding the attainment of goals.

Cultivating Integrity in Growth Hacking

Building integrity in growth hacking requires a commitment to excellence, accountability, and ethical conduct in all aspects of the journey. It involves setting high standards for oneself and holding oneself accountable for upholding those standards, even in the face of challenges or setbacks. Embracing wholeheartedness, individuals infuse their work with integrity, authenticity, and purpose, driving innovation and success in their endeavors.

Upholding Ethical Standards

Integrity in growth hacking also entails upholding ethical standards and moral integrity in all interactions and decisions.
It means acting with honesty, transparency, and integrity, even when faced with difficult choices or temptations.

Hence, prioritizing ethical conduct and moral integrity, individuals build trust, credibility, and respect within their teams and communities, fostering a culture of integrity and accountability that fuels growth and innovation.

Leading by Example

As leaders in the field of growth hacking, individuals have a responsibility to lead by example and inspire others to embrace integrity and wholeheartedness in their work and interactions. By demonstrating a commitment to excellence, authenticity, and ethical conduct, leaders create a culture of integrity and accountability that empowers teams to achieve greatness and make a positive impact in the world.

Integrity is the foundation of growth hacking success, anchoring individuals in authenticity, accountability, and ethical conduct. By embracing wholeheartedness and avoiding half-hearted efforts, individuals infuse their work with integrity, passion, and purpose, driving innovation and success in the dynamic world of growth hacking. As they cultivate integrity in their endeavors, may they always remember the transformative power of wholeheartedness to inspire greatness, foster trust, and propel them towards their goals and aspirations.

Till Growth Do Us Part: Embracing a Lifelong Commitment to Personal and Professional Development

In the journey of life and career, growth emerges as a constant companion, guiding individuals towards self-discovery, fulfillment, and success. This chapter explores the concept of marrying growth till death do us part, emphasizing the importance of embracing a lifelong commitment to personal and professional development.

The Journey of Growth

Growth is not a destination but a journey, a continuous process of self-discovery, learning, and evolution. From the moment we are born until the end of our lives, growth accompanies us, presenting opportunities for exploration, transformation, and expansion. Embracing growth means embracing change, uncertainty, and the unknown, and trusting in the power of learning and adaptation to navigate the complexities of life and career.

Commitment to Personal Development

Marrying growth till death do us part involves a commitment to personal development and self-improvement. It means embracing a mindset of curiosity, openness, and resilience, and actively seeking out opportunities for growth and learning in every aspect of life. Whether it's acquiring new skills, pursuing passions and interests, or overcoming challenges and obstacles, individuals committed to personal development are dedicated to becoming the best version of themselves and maximizing their potential for success and fulfillment.

Cultivating Professional Growth

Professional growth is an essential component of marrying growth till death do us part, as individuals navigate the ever-changing landscape of career and work. It involves setting ambitious goals, pursuing new opportunities, and continuously expanding one's knowledge, expertise, and network.

By embracing professional growth, individuals position themselves for success and advancement, seizing opportunities for career progression, innovation, and impact in their chosen fields.

Embracing Lifelong Learning

At the heart of marrying growth till death do us part lies a commitment to lifelong learning. Lifelong learning is the key to staying relevant, adaptable, and resilient in an increasingly complex and dynamic world. It involves seeking out new experiences, perspectives, and knowledge, and being open to growth and change at every stage of life. By embracing lifelong learning, individuals enrich their lives, broaden their horizons, and cultivate a sense of purpose and meaning that transcends age, status, or circumstance.

Navigating Challenges and Setbacks

Marrying growth till death do us part requires resilience and determination in the face of challenges and setbacks. It means embracing failure as an opportunity for learning and growth and refusing to be deterred by obstacles or setbacks along the way. By adopting a growth mindset and viewing challenges as opportunities for growth and self-improvement, individuals can overcome adversity and emerge stronger, wiser, and more resilient than before.

Celebrating Milestones and Achievements

Throughout the journey of marrying growth till death do us part, it's important to celebrate milestones and achievements along the way. Whether it's mastering a new skill, achieving a long-held goal, or reaching a significant milestone in one's personal or professional life, celebrating achievements reinforces the value of growth and motivates individuals to continue striving for excellence and fulfillment in all areas of life.

Marrying growth till death do us part is a lifelong commitment to personal and professional development, embracing change, learning, and evolution at every stage of life.

With the urge to embrace growth as a constant companion and navigate the journey with curiosity, resilience, and determination, individuals can unlock their full potential and create a life filled with purpose, passion, and fulfilment. As they embark on this lifelong journey of growth, may they always remember the transformative power of growth to enrich their lives and make a positive impact in the world.

Periodic Measurement of Genuine Progress: Navigating the Growth Journey with Clarity and Purpose

In the pursuit of growth hacking excellence, progress is not merely about moving forward but also about ensuring that each step taken is meaningful, impactful, and aligned with one's goals and aspirations. This chapter explores the importance of measuring genuine progress periodically, emphasizing the need for clarity, accountability, and purpose in the dynamic world of growth hacking.

The Significance of Genuine Progress

Genuine progress goes beyond surface-level achievements or superficial metrics; it encompasses meaningful growth and development that aligns with one's values, vision, and purpose. It involves making strides towards tangible goals and objectives, while also cultivating personal and professional growth, resilience, and well-being.

Genuine progress is the foundation upon which success, fulfillment, and impact are built in the journey of growth hacking.

Setting Clear Objectives and Key Results (OKRs)

Periodic measurement of genuine progress begins with setting clear objectives and key results (OKRs) that provide a roadmap for success and guide individuals toward their desired outcomes. OKRs help individuals define specific, measurable, achievable, relevant, and time-bound goals, as well as establish key metrics and milestones to track progress along the way. By aligning actions with objectives and key results, individuals ensure that their efforts are focused, purposeful, and directed towards meaningful outcomes.

Tracking Key Metrics and Indicators

Measuring genuine progress periodically involves tracking key metrics and indicators that provide insights into performance, effectiveness, and impact.

These metrics may include quantitative data such as revenue growth, customer acquisition, or product adoption rates, as well as qualitative indicators such as customer satisfaction, employee engagement, or brand reputation.

By regularly monitoring key metrics and indicators, individuals can assess their progress, identify areas for improvement, and make informed decisions to optimize their efforts and maximize their impact.

Reflecting on Lessons Learned

Periodic measurement of genuine progress also entails reflecting on lessons learned and leveraging insights to inform future actions and decisions.

Reflection allows individuals to evaluate their successes and failures, identify patterns and trends, and extract valuable learnings that contribute to personal and professional growth.

By embracing a mindset of continuous learning and improvement, individuals can adapt to changing circumstances, overcome challenges, and refine their strategies for greater success and impact in the journey of growth hacking.

Adjusting Course as Needed

Measuring genuine progress periodically empowers individuals to adjust course as needed and pivot in response to new information, emerging trends, or shifting priorities.

Flexibility and adaptability are essential qualities in the dynamic world of growth hacking, where agility and innovation are paramount.

Make sure to regularly assess their progress and course-correcting as needed, individuals can stay responsive to changes in the environment, seize growth opportunities, and navigate the complexities of the journey with clarity, purpose, and resilience.

Celebrating Milestones and Achievements

Periodic measurement of genuine progress provides opportunities to celebrate milestones and achievements along the way.

Celebrating successes reinforces motivation, morale, and momentum, and fosters a sense of accomplishment and pride in one's efforts.

By acknowledging and celebrating progress, individuals cultivate a positive mindset, boost confidence, and fuel their drive to continue striving for excellence and impact in the journey of growth hacking.

Measuring genuine progress periodically is essential for navigating the journey of growth hacking with clarity, purpose, and intentionality. By setting clear objectives and key results, tracking key metrics and indicators, reflecting on lessons learned, adjusting course as needed, and celebrating milestones and achievements, individuals ensure that their efforts are focused, purposeful, and directed towards meaningful outcomes. As they embrace the practice of periodic measurement of genuine progress, may they navigate the complexities of the growth hacking journey with confidence, resilience, and a relentless pursuit of excellence and impact.

The Acid Test of Growth Hacking: Sizzle with Your Work or Pivot for Growth

In the dynamic world of growth hacking, success hinges on one's ability to not only innovate but also to continually reassess and adapt to changing circumstances. This chapter explores the acid test of growth hacking: if you don't sizzle with your work or person, then it's time to pivot for growth.

Embracing the Growth Hacking Acid Test

The acid test serves as a litmus test for individuals to evaluate their alignment with their work or personal pursuits. If one does not feel a sense of excitement, passion, or fulfillment in their endeavors, it may indicate a need for change or adaptation. In the fast-paced environment of growth hacking, where innovation and agility are paramount, the acid test provides a valuable framework for assessing one's readiness to pivot and pursue new growth opportunities.

Recognizing the Signs

Several signs may indicate a lack of sizzle in one's work or personal life. These may include feelings of boredom, disengagement, or stagnation, as well as a lack of enthusiasm or passion for one's daily activities.

He also notice a disconnect between their values, interests, and aspirations, and the demands or expectations of their current role or environment.

Recognizing these signs is the first step towards acknowledging the need for change and embracing the acid test of growth hacking.

Embracing the Pivot

When faced with the realization that they don't sizzle with their work or person, individuals have the opportunity to pivot and pursue new opportunities for growth and fulfillment. This may involve making a career change, starting a new venture, or embarking on a personal journey of exploration and self-discovery. By embracing the pivot, individuals can harness the power of change to reignite their passion, purpose, and sense of possibility, propelling them towards new levels of success and fulfilment.

Leveraging the Growth Mindset

The acid test of growth hacking is rooted in the growth mindset, a belief that intelligence and abilities can be developed through effort, practice, and learning.

My friend who embrace the growth mindset view challenges and setbacks as opportunities for growth and self-improvement, rather than barriers to success.

By adopting this mindset, individuals can approach the acid test with curiosity, resilience, and a willingness to explore new possibilities for growth and transformation.

Cultivating Resilience and Adaptability

Navigating the acid test of growth hacking requires resilience and adaptability in the face of uncertainty and change. Individuals must be willing to let go of what no longer serves them and embrace the unknown with courage and openness. By cultivating resilience and adaptability, individuals can navigate the ups and downs of the growth-hacking journey with grace and confidence, knowing that each pivot brings them closer to their goals and aspirations.

The acid test of growth hacking serves as a powerful tool for individuals to assess their alignment with their work or personal pursuits and embrace new opportunities for growth and fulfillment. By recognizing the signs that they don't sizzle with their work or person, individuals can leverage the power of the pivot to reignite their passion, purpose, and sense of possibility. As they navigate the complexities of the growth hacking journey, may they always remember that change is not only inevitable but also an essential catalyst for innovation, evolution, and growth.

Harnessing the Power of Brain Mapping for Periodic Progress Evaluation

In the journey of growth hacking, periodic evaluation of progress is essential for staying on track, adapting strategies, and achieving desired outcomes. This chapter explores the significance of using brain mapping techniques to visualize and analyze progress periodically, providing valuable insights and guidance for individuals navigating the dynamic world of growth hacking.

Understanding Brain Mapping

Brain mapping is a powerful technique that allows individuals to visualize and analyze their thoughts, behaviors, and decision-making processes. By mapping neural pathways and cognitive patterns, individuals gain valuable insights into how they perceive, process, and respond to information and stimuli. Brain mapping techniques may include mind mapping, cognitive mapping, or neuro-imaging technologies such as functional magnetic resonance imaging (fMRI) or electroencephalography (EEG).

Visualising Progress with Mind Mapping

Mind mapping is a popular brain mapping technique that enables individuals to visualize their thoughts, ideas, and goals in a structured and interconnected format. By creating a visual representation of their progress, individuals can identify patterns, connections, and areas for improvement, as well as track milestones and achievements over time. Mind mapping serves as a valuable tool for periodic progress evaluation, providing clarity, focus, and direction in the journey of growth hacking.

Analysing Cognitive Patterns with Cognitive Mapping

Cognitive mapping involves analyzing cognitive patterns and mental processes to gain insights into how individuals perceive and interpret information. By mapping cognitive structures and connections, individuals can identify biases, assumptions, and cognitive shortcuts that may influence their decision-making and behavior. Cognitive mapping helps individuals become more self-aware and reflective, enabling them to make informed choices and adapt strategies based on a deeper understanding of their thought processes.

Leveraging Neuro-imaging Technologies for Insights

Neuro-imaging technologies such as functional magnetic resonance imaging (fMRI) and electroencephalography (EEG) provide valuable insights into brain activity and neural functioning. By measuring brain activity in real time, these technologies offer objective data on how individuals respond to stimuli, make decisions, and process information. Neuro-imaging can complement traditional brain mapping techniques, providing a more comprehensive understanding of the cognitive mechanisms underlying progress evaluation and decision-making in the context of growth hacking.

Integrating Brain Mapping into Periodic Progress Evaluation

Integrating brain mapping techniques into periodic progress evaluation enables individuals to gain a deeper understanding of their growth hacking efforts and outcomes. By visualizing progress, analyzing cognitive patterns, and leveraging neuro-imaging technologies, individuals can identify strengths, weaknesses, and opportunities for improvement, as well as make data-driven decisions to optimize their strategies and maximize their impact. Brain mapping serves as a powerful tool for enhancing self-awareness, decision-making, and performance in the journey of growth hacking.

The managing director is pioneering a groundbreaking approach by integrating brain mapping into periodic progress evaluations.

This innovative technique involves analyzing employees' neural responses to various tasks and challenges, providing insights into their cognitive functions and emotional well-being. By incorporating brain mapping, the director aims to enhance the accuracy and depth of performance assessments, identifying not only areas for improvement but also untapped potential. This method fosters a more holistic understanding of each team member's capabilities, leading to personalized development plans and optimized team dynamics. Ultimately, this forward-thinking strategy promises to drive greater efficiency, innovation, and job satisfaction within the organization.

Brain mapping techniques offer valuable insights and guidance for individuals navigating the complexities of the growth hacking journey. By visualizing progress, analyzing cognitive patterns, and leveraging neuro-imaging technologies, individuals gain a deeper understanding of their thought processes, behaviors, and decision-making mechanisms, enabling them to make informed choices and adapt strategies for greater success and impact. As they integrate brain mapping into periodic progress evaluation, may they harness the power of self-awareness and data-driven decision-making to achieve their goals and aspirations in the dynamic world of growth hacking.

Simplicity in Strategic Thinking: The Key to Success

In the fast-paced and often chaotic world of business and decision-making, there is a prevailing myth that complexity equates to sophistication and success. This myth leads many to believe that elaborate strategies, filled with intricate details and multiple contingencies, are the hallmarks of effective leadership and management. However, reality often tells a different story. The most successful strategies are frequently characterized by their simplicity. This chapter explores why simplicity in strategic thinking is not only advantageous but essential, and how embracing simplicity can lead to clarity, efficiency, and sustainable success.

The Power of Simplicity

Simplicity in strategic thinking means distilling a strategy down to its core essence, focusing on the most critical elements, and eliminating unnecessary complications. This approach offers several compelling advantages:

1. **Clarity and Focus:** Simplicity brings clarity. When a strategy is simple, it is easier to communicate, understand, and execute. Clear and focused strategies enable teams to align their efforts and work towards common goals without confusion or misdirection.
2. **Agility and Adaptability:** Simple strategies are more flexible and adaptable to changing circumstances. Complexity often results in rigidity, making it difficult to pivot when new opportunities or threats arise. A simple strategy, on the other hand, allows for quick adjustments and responsiveness.
3. **Resource Efficiency:** Resources, whether time, money, or personnel, are finite. Simple strategies optimize resource allocation by concentrating efforts on the most impactful activities. This prevents the dispersion of resources across too many initiatives, which can dilute effectiveness.
4. **Enhanced Decision-Making:** Simplified strategies facilitate better decision-making. When decision-makers are not bogged down by excessive details and convoluted plans, they can focus on critical issues, make quicker decisions, and implement actions more effectively.
5. **Sustainability:** Overly complex strategies can be unsustainable in the long run. They often require continuous monitoring, adjustments, and resources that can strain an organization. Simple strategies, being more straightforward and manageable, are easier to maintain and scale over time.

Simplicity in strategic thinking is not about dumbing down or oversimplifying complex issues. It is about honing in on what truly matters, and making strategic decisions that are clear, focused, and executable. In a world where complexity is often mistaken for competence, embracing simplicity can set you apart, driving greater clarity, agility, and sustainable success.

Remember, you have everything you need; the key lies in cleaning away the unnecessary and focusing on the essence of your simplicity in strategic thinking for growth hacking.

Dear Reader,

A Blessing for Your Journey

As you embark on the journey of growth hacking, may you be surrounded by blessings and good fortune at every turn. This concluding chapter is a heartfelt wish for your success and fulfilment in all aspects of your venture.

Embracing Abundance
May abundance flow effortlessly into your life and venture, bringing prosperity, success, and abundance in all forms. May you attract wealth, opportunities, and resources that support your growth hacking endeavors and enable you to make a positive impact in the world.

Pursuing Success with Integrity
May you achieve success with integrity, authenticity, and ethical conduct. May you uphold high standards of honesty, transparency, and accountability in all your interactions and decisions, and may your integrity be a guiding light that leads you to greatness and fulfilment.

Advancing Spirituality and Well-Being
May your journey of growth hacking not only lead to external success but also to inner fulfillment and spiritual growth. May you cultivate mindfulness, presence, and gratitude in your daily life, and may you find peace, joy, and serenity amidst the busyness of your endeavors.

Finding Happiness and Fulfilment
May you find happiness and fulfillment in the pursuit of your goals and aspirations. May you embrace the journey with enthusiasm, passion, and purpose, and may you savor every moment of progress, learning, and achievement along the way.

Wishing You Wealth and Prosperity
May you be blessed with abundance and prosperity beyond your wildest dreams. May you achieve financial freedom, security, and independence, and may you use your wealth and resources to create positive change and uplift those in need.

Final Blessings
As you venture forth into the world of growth hacking, may you be
surrounded by blessings, guidance, and support every step of the way. May
you overcome obstacles with courage, resilience, and grace, and may you
emerge stronger, wiser, and more empowered than ever before.

Remember, you have everything you need; the key lies in cleaning away
the unnecessary thoughts and focusing on the essence of your simplicity in
strategic thinking for growth hacking.

Best of luck for hacking growth. Be a millionaire, be successful, advance
spirituality, enjoy happiness and wealth. You have the power within you to
achieve greatness, and may your journey be filled with blessings,
abundance, and endless possibilities.

Dr Nilesh Pawaskar

Quotes by Dr Nilesh Pawaskar

"Simple is scalable"

"Personal growth is professional growth hacking"

"Humility is giving up social importance in the business circle that makes you special"

"Being Sudama, Each friend in our lives plays role of Krishna"

"They wanted me to be 'Diamond' but I decided to be 'GOLD' to hold many diamonds in jewelry"

"Each song is a devotional piece with spiritual connection"

"Doing nothing is the best strategy"

"Everything is untrue, it is perishable"

This book Spiritual guide for growth